For You I Remember

By

Edith Bishop

GOURDAS HOUSE, PUBLISHERS
ABERDEEN
1980

To my sister Gladys who for many years was my constant girlhood companion and shared with me many delightful ploys and adventures.

FIRST PUBLISHED 1980
by Gourdas House, Publishers
5 Alford Place, Aberdeen

ISBN 0 907301 01 0

Printed in Great Britain by
Clark Constable Ltd. Edinburgh

For You I Remember

Contents

	Page
Introduction	9
28th November 1896	11
My Mother	12
My Father	16
At Ashley Road School	19
On Ashley Road	22
At Home	26
Housework Then	34
Entertainments Then	39
To Greensyde	43
At Kittybrewster School	45
Memories of Thought Reading and Mother's Spiritualism	50
My Holidays at Newburgh	55
First Meeting — Davie	63
At the Central School	69
The War Continues	77
At the Training Centre	80
The Land Girls	85
The Demonstration School	92
Davie Again	95
The War Is Over	99
8th September 1920	101

List of Illustrations

	Page
My Father	30
Edith and Gladys with their nanny	31
Edith (age 3) and Gladys (age $4\frac{1}{2}$)	32
My Mother	33
Edith in party dress (age 10)	49
The boys at Gordon's Woodie 1912	67
Central School hockey team 1914	68
Edith, in her late teens	75
4th Gordon Highlanders Territorial camp at Tain	76
Edith as Princess Crystal in the operetta 'The Sleeping Princess' at the Training Centre	79
The Land Girls	84
The Land Girls again	91
Davie	97
Edith	98

The Publisher gratefully acknowledges the assistance of Aberdonians George Muiry and John McIntosh for their re-creation of the photographs used for these illustrations.

Introduction

Edith Bishop was three years old when Queen Victoria died — seven years old when Orville and Wilbur Wright got off the ground and into the air at Kitty Hawk — fifteen years old when the Titanic sank in the North Atlantic and a young woman of seventeen when the Great War erupted over Europe.

Born at a time when Britain had her Empire — the Boer War and the Klondyke Gold Rush just on the horizon and the spirit of adventure being fired by expeditions contemplating the North and South Poles — it is perhaps difficult to grasp the scene of some eighty years ago.

The 'Aberdeen Evening Express' of 31st December, 1896 makes fascinating reading. Then, Edith Bishop would have been just a month old. The advertisements surprise the eye. A bottle of whisky for 2/6, — a ton of 'Finest Hetton Coal' for 19/6 — and a bicycle! What a selection. Cycling would appear to have been the popular thing then. You are advised to inspect the 'Royal Caledonian Cycle', a sound, well finished cycle at medium price of £12–10/- or why not try the 'Rudge Whitworth quadruplet' — a cycle for FOUR RIDERS! Also in that Hogmanay edition the leading article summarised some of the events of the past year. Perhaps an extract from these columns will help create a back drop to start Edith Bishop's story.

> On the whole, 1896 has been a humdrum sort of year. It cannot be looked upon as a bad year, for trade and commerce have been distinctly healthy; still, it cannot be ranked as a year of great things that might make it stand out in history with any degree of prominence. True, we have had the marvellous discovery, the Röngten rays, and the formal inauguration of the motor car; England has been visited by a shock of earthquake, and a huge bog has slipped

> its moorings in Ireland; a great political party has lost its leader, and Nansen has come home after having pierced within 260 miles of the North Pole; and we have been visited by Li Hung Chang and the Emperor of Russia; yet all these events combined are not sufficient to mark 1896 as a record year. Nor has literature or art given the world anything strikingly new; while, as to science, with the exception of the 'X' rays' discovery, nothing has occurred of any great moment. . . .
>
> And how has the year dealt with our own braif toon? Fairly well on the whole. It has been in every sense of the word a developing year. Our leading industries have progressed; that unfailing index of prosperity — the harbour revenue — has shown a remarkable advance; building has been prosperous; the fishing industry has been very well maintained; the granite trade has been fairly brisk; and employment for all classes of workers has been exceedingly good. There have been no great schemes of improvement inaugurated, but the town is none the worse of a rest in that respect. It does not always answer to be continually turning the town upside down. . . .

Late in the November of that year, where, in Aberdeen, most peoples' thoughts were turning to the coming Christmas, there was one family whose thoughts were preoccupied with the imminent arrival of a baby. Would it be a boy or a girl — a time honoured question. It was a girl, christened Edith McLean. Now, over eighty years later she looks back and gives us a glimpse of her life and her experiences at the turn of the century to her marriage in 1920. For you she remembers.

28th November 1896

The hansom cab spanked along the quiet street of terraced and semi-detached granite houses of Ashley Road. The driver, perched on his high seat, urged his horse, then drew up quickly at Number 60 and a gentleman hastily emerged. He was elegantly attired in morning coat and tile hat. After pulling out the brass knob which sent a bell ting-a-linging in the kitchen of the house, he drew off his kid gloves.

A maid opened the door and after depositing hat and gloves on the hall-stand, the gentleman hastened upstairs to the bedroom where mother-to-be and nurse awaited doctor to deliver the baby — ME!

Happily this did not take long, nor was there any cry until my first on this earth, as my mother was blessed with remarkable ability to produce babies without pain. She had five in all. I was the second, my sister Gladys being 19 months older.

The doctor will not have forgotten her birth. He visited Mother as she thought the birth was imminent, examined her and said it would be some time yet. As he went down the stairs, he heard her laughing and joking with the nurse. Just as he was about to enter his carriage, he heard a shout to come back and dashed upstairs to find the baby born! 'My God!' was all he could stammer.

This is a good introduction to Mother, as all her long life of wonderful good health, she managed to have the fun with little of the pain.

My Mother

Mother's father was a McLeod, and her mother Irish. She used to tell us she was related to the 'Russells of Aden'. Her grandmother eloped with a footman and they were ostracised by the family. As a little girl, she remembered two 'Russell ladies' visiting. They arrived in a carriage and had beautiful dresses of stiff silk. She was told that they owned a back-gammon table that used to belong to Lord Byron.

She never knew her own mother or any of her mother's people as her mother left her father when she was very young. She often wished she could find her mother and her sister who was a baby at that time.

Grandfather went to Nova Scotia and eventually married again. Mother had nothing but praise for Almira, her stepmother. I never saw either, but we were often reminded of them by lovely presents. He was a jeweller so we were lucky to have some nice bangles, necklaces, brooches and watches. But for Christmas — always a huge barrel of apples, one half bright reds and the other greeny yellows. On one occasion I saw the lorry approaching with the barrel well in evidence. I rushed into the house shouting, 'The barrel of apples is came, the barrel of apples is came!'

For a few years Mother was educated at a boarding school in the south of England, then was brought up by her aunts Sharah — 'Sadie' and Elizabeth — 'Betsy' who lived in King Street. A cousin, Chris McLeod, also stayed there. Sadie was Infant Mistress at Hanover Street School when Father was headmaster. That was how Mother met Father.

Every summer holiday Mother sailed to Nova Scotia to be with her father and stepmother. One time she returned a little earlier than was expected. She went to Hanover Street School, watched till the Headmaster's room was vacant, then slipped in. She hid behind a cupboard and when Father appeared and was busy with papers, she sprang out. Father got a terrible shock — thinking she was still in Nova Scotia. That settled it! They became engaged!

Mother was the most stagestruck person I have ever come across. Had she been reared in an atmosphere less antagonistic to the career of an actress, there's no doubt she would have been one. Often a teenager will have a great fancy for what she takes to be the glamorous life of the stage, and then gets over it, like most youthful crushes. But Mother — no. It was part of her nature. All her life, nothing was so marvellous to her as the Stage, professionals were the cream of the earth, and acting and singing the most wonderful thing you could do.

In a way, mysterious to me, she got to know many people in the profession, or allied to it somehow, and many gay evenings we had with them and her ragtime band. Mother had great strength of character, disarming charm and terrific powers of persuasion. That was how she managed so often to come out victorious when Father objected to any of her ploys, as also did some critical people in the teaching profession, and serious folk in the kirk.

Yes, Mother gave 'Mother Grundy' something to speak about in Aberdeen. And when I think of it now! Most of her goings on would not turn a hair in this permissive age; in fact she would be counted rather wonderful.

Mother caused gossip about what nowadays would be thought very tame conduct indeed. Occasionally she liked to have a cup of tea down town at the Westend Cafe in Union Street. Now, believe it or not, by some people at that time it was counted not quite respectable for a married woman to be going to a cafe all by herself! In any case Mother was very friendly with the manageress, Fanny Gordon.

Another matter which set tongues wagging was Mother's racial discrimination; but with her, it was the opposite to the usual. She thought any other race to be superior to our own. The result was that foreigners loomed largely in her friendships. In her tennis club at one time I can remember French, Belgian, Swedish, Jewish, Ceylonese, Japanese, Chinese, West Indian and German people; and the Roman Catholic Club next to ours supplied two friendly priests, one Irish.

A class of people greatly admired by Mother was artists. She, herself, sketched, and belonged to a Sketching Club. This also was counted not quite the thing to do. Tut-tut! Going away to these lonely places to sketch!

But, dear, oh dear! when she cut her hair! 'Have you heard? Mrs. McLean has cut her hair! Yes, just like a boy! What they call 'a bob' . . . disgraceful . . . a headmaster's wife!' I have been told that Mother was the first in Aberdeen to have her hair bobbed — avant garde with a vengeance!

The illogicality of these comments was that those who had long hair often put it up in the most artificial way, inserting large pads like loofahs with the hair over them, pinning curls on the top of that and perhaps a pleat fixed round as well. Then there were fancy hair slides and Spanish combs with glittering designs.

Perched on top of all that would be a huge brimmed hat trimmed with a mass of flowers or large ostrich feathers, each made from a few ordinary ostrich feathers. The final result was sometimes of such grandiose proportions that the lady had to bend her head carefully to the side before she could enter a tram!

This was the time also of the hobble skirt which was so tight at the foot you couldn't walk at all had it not been for a little slit. Even so — you couldn't walk — just hobble. The popular song went:

> Oh, the hobble, the horrible, horrible hobble,
> Chase me, Charlie, the boys will catch me now.
> For it's baggy round the middle
> And tighter down below,
> And the boys are disappointed
> When the wind begins to blow.

Add to the huge hat, the horrible hobble and I'll leave to your imagination the picture of a lady mounting a tram!

No wonder Mother felt like a prisoner set free, when she had her hair cut, and perhaps a little skittish like a newly shorn sheep. That was exactly my feeling when mine was done!

I had a tremendous head of auburn hair. It had responded magnificently to the careful treatment when I was a girl. It was thick and so long I could sit on it. It required a mountain of pins to keep it in order — most uncomfortable — and I could seldom find a hat which did not grip my forehead causing headaches. It was a great asset for theatricals when playing such parts as Miranda, or singing in Operettas such as Princess Crystal, but otherwise a trial and a time waster.

Mother had a rich mezzo soprano voice of fine quality and she loved romantic ballads, musical comedies, Gilbert and Sullivan and Johann Strauss. She could play the piano well enough to put in accompaniments to most of these. We always had the full book of whatever musical was popular at the time. As the family grew older you could hear choruses and solos coming happily from Greensyde nearly every day. I inherited a liking for all these songs as well as a mezzo voice.

My Father

My Father, William David McLean, F.E.I.S., was orphaned early in life. His father was in the Police force at Kirriemuir, coming there from Ullapool. I believe I still have relatives in that district. As a young boy, Father was at school with James Barrie, his home being adjacent to Barrie's. He told me the first real football he ever saw was one which Barrie produced after a visit to Edinburgh.

He was a wonderful headmaster. Although these were the days of much administration of the tawse, he seldom wielded it. His overpowering personality did the trick. His step in the corridor was the signal for all pupils in a class to 'sit up' and be on their best behaviour.

He also was an excellent teacher. Every school was the better for his sojourn as Head; the Inspector's marks for every subject going up and up. His speciality was 'Writing' — copperplate. By the time a pupil reached the qualifying class he could write copperplate. Father demonstrated his method to each teacher, who carried it out with enthusiasm. I have seen essays and dictations of a whole class, every single one in this beautiful writing.

Anyone seeing the hen's scrawls which today I put on paper, would never guess that at one time I also could produce this; moreover, I could teach it. This makes me wonder how important it really is, learning to write copperplate when, as in my case, under the pressure of making speedy notes, it gradually deteriorates. Certainly modern educationists count it wasted effort. But, perhaps it kept my writing from being worse, even becoming illegible! The importance of writing does seem to be waning now we have typewriters, tape recorders and telephones.

I will always remember Father being a wonderful bedside story teller — usually of the Red Indian — Buffalo Bill variety — and stage coaches attacked by highwaymen.

Father's personal sports were swimming, tennis, cricket, boating, trout-fishing and golf. He was a keen mountaineer at a time when it was not as popular as it is today. He belonged to the Thick Skin Cricket Club which had an annual outing to the Brig o' Potarch Hotel, Deeside, which has a large, green park beside the River Dee amidst beautiful surroundings.

Father was also keen on sports for the young, and won shields for boys' and girls' teams of bar-bells, dumb-bells and Indian clubs. He introduced the teaching of swimming in Aberdeen schools, starting with his own, Hanover Street. The swimming as well as the first Medical Inspection of Schools disclosed that a few children were 'sewn up' for the winter. Their clothes could not come off at all! The next school to have swimming was Frederick Street, and the first inter-school swimming gala was between these schools.

Although I was then just about five years old, I shall never forget this event and the tremendous excitement we children had. The Baths at the Beach were packed, children in the gallery, and adults and guests seated round the edge of the pond with towels spread over knees to avoid the effects of salt water splashing. The noise of shouting and cheering, augmented by the echo of the building, would have vied with the roar of a Cup Final.

But neither shall I forget seeing the rows of dangling feet round the gallery. A good proportion were bare. Let us not forget, when we talk of poverty, that even the poorest families today are so much better off than were those children of the unemployed and low wage earners of the period before the 1914–18 war. 'Soup Kitchens' provided for the needy a mid-day meal of a large bowl of soup and a huge roll — almost as large as some of the tiny, thin faces. Father always had a supply of boots and shoes in a cupboard, donated by the church and friends.

Father was strictly brought up to be a devoted member of the United Free Church of Scotland and, like all strong believers of a particular form of faith, he held the firm opinion that his Church and his Church alone was the right one. It was not long till he was an elder.

All elders who served at Communion wore morning 'frock' coats and tile hats. I used to love to get to open the stiff box, shaped like a big hat, where the tile reposed on a rack which prevented the glistening sides from touching the box. Carefully I would take the hat out and find at the foot of the box the soft velvet pad with which to skiff it round and round till not a tuft was out of place — a work of art! The difficult parts were the crown and the up-turned brim. Sometimes we heated the pad slightly for better effect, or used a silk handkerchief. What care, what superlative care had then to be taken to keep it in this immaculate condition. One little scuff the wrong way could spoil it! When the elders took up position round the communion table, it was an impressive and awesome sight.

Father gave himself to the Church. He visited the members of his district regularly, paying special attention to any who were ill. He was President of the Band of Hope and of the Literary and Debating Society. He taught a 'Welfare of Youth' class, many of his pupils gaining distinction, one being first in Scotland. He gave 'papers' on various subjects such as Robert Louis Stevenson, of whom he was an ardent admirer, or Shakespeare who, along with Napoleon, were his special studies.

Father certainly tried to bring up his family not only to know the Scriptures, but also the Shorter Catechism. We attended morning service, afternoon Sunday School, and evening service every Sunday, also the Band of Hope on Friday evenings. We had at least one and a half miles to walk to the South Church. Even when tram cars ran part of the way, we were not allowed to board one, that would have been sinful, forcing someone to work on Sunday.

At Ashley Road School

I was given to understand that I was a very good-natured child, but on one occasion I broke out and made a terrific scene. When my sister Gladys was five years old past April, she was due to go to school in August. Ashley Road School was just about 200 yards from our home at Number 60 on the other side of the road and, although I was only three years nine months old, I was determined to go too.

So I pleaded, argued, howled and wept until victory was mine. 'Let her go, she'll soon come back', they said. But did she? No. She simply loved it. In a way, my Father came to feel rather proud of it — being a headmaster!

Ashley Road School was like all Public Schools in Aberdeen — co-educational. It differed in only one way; a small fee was charged — but very small. All the other Public Schools were free.

By today's standards the classes were large. The only way to teach in these circumstances was by keeping good discipline and making certain the children paid attention to what the teacher said. We chanted out many things — which we loved to do. All children are fond of rhythm and remember what they learn in this way. It is the most pleasant method of teaching facts which have to be memorised, and you can not get away from having to memorise — starting with the alphabet.

It is nonsense to say, as many modern educationists do, that if you make a child understand, it is not necessary to memorise. We live by our memory. Every experience is in the past by the time we are conscious of it. Memory should be trained and can be trained.

Although co-educational in class, the girls and boys had separate playgrounds and entrances. A master tolled a huge bell, and sometimes blew a whistle, which was the signal for us to line up in our separate classes and march in. This we also liked to do. There's something about marching!

At playtime we had a great variety of games. Tick-and-tack, Rounders, Bobbies and Thieves, Cowboys and Indians, Hoist the Flag, French Cricket, Skipping Ropes, Beddies, Spinning Tops, Marbles (Bools), Hoops and Iron Girds, and Walking on Stilts.

We also had singing games such as 'The Farmer's in the Yard', when we finished by clapping the dog, or 'In and out the Windows' which finished by going to London. But I think the favourite was 'Little Sally Walker sitting in the sun'.

Little Sally Walker, sitting in the sun,
Crying and weeping for a young man.
Rise, Sally Walker, wipe away your tears,
Choose from the East or choose from the West,
Choose the very one that you love best.

In the winter we made long slides requiring a good power of balance to negotiate. A few lucky ones had skates and little sledges. We built snowmen and had snowball fights. There was an exciting feud with Broomhill School. We made piles of snowball ammunition. When round the corner of Great Western Road and Ashley Road the Broomhillites came charging with fierce yells, the 'Charge of the Light Brigade' wasn't in it. There was a seething melee. I am sure many a friend was hit instead of an enemy.

Sometimes deep snow lay for a few weeks and the school had double attendances, i.e. a half hour interval at lunchtime and dismissed about half past two in the afternoon. Most children had a 'piece' to tide them over till reaching home, but Sangster, the baker, in the happy position of being opposite the school, laid on a special feast at low price — hot Bovril and pies. Although our home was just a few doors up from Sangster, Gladys and I were determined not to miss the treat and joined the happy throng there.

Three subjects at Ashley Road School were fee-paying — Gymnastics, Dancing and Piano playing. Gladys and I took the three and enjoyed them all. It added to the enjoyment that we got off ordinary class work to do so. Gladys excelled at dancing and gym. I've no doubt this helped her when later on she became a ballet dancer and still later on a golf champion of Royal Blackheath Golf Club.

Dancing was taught by a very experienced gentleman, Cosmo Mitchell, and a pianist was there to accompany our steps. The dances taught were Waltz, Valetta Waltz, Circassian Circle, Polka, Lancers, Quadrilles, Highland Scottische, Eightsome Reel and Foursome Reel. For step-dancing, we had Highland Fling, Sword Dance, Seann Trews, Cake Walk and Skirt Dance. For this last very special and pretty one, our skirts were ten yards wide and accordian pleated. These had also to be our party dresses for a few years.

I remember the melodies played for all these dances. The Cake Walk was 'When we are married, we'll have sausages for tea'. At that time every dance started with the Grand March and Circassian Circle which mixed the dancers in a friendly way.

We had a visiting teacher of singing. He had a small organ which could be taken from one classroom to another, and a modulator to teach 'Doh, ray, me'. First was Mr. Lister and I cannot refrain from letting you know a rhyme which we used to sing delightedly:

Mr. Lister had a blister
On his great big toe.
Mr. Lister burst his blister
Singing 'Doh, ray, me, fa, soh'.

Then it was Charles Soutar, who was to be my school singing master till the end of my schooldays.

Gladys and I both came on well at the piano and played some duets. For one, 'Sleigh Ride' we had elastic bracelets with bells on our wrists which jingled delightfully in time to the music.

On Ashley Road

We children each got a Saturday penny and could purchase a variety of sweets with it. Black sugar stripes, sherbet dabs, jaw-pullers, bull's eyes, chewing gum and jelly babies, being amongst the most popular. But there were marzipan potatoes which had the additional attraction of perhaps containing a lucky half-penny inside! The jaw-puller was a long, thin slab of candy which certainly pulled your jaws while eating. It stuck and stuck, lasting a blissfully long time. Here the extra bonus was a thin, circular tin disc with holes through which a double length of twine was drawn. You held the double string at each side, keeping the two lengths of string apart with two fingers and whirled the disc round and round till the string was well twisted. Then, miracle! You pulled it out and in while the disc whizzed and hummed; out and in, out and in, making a lively, whining noise. You could go on for ever! See-saw, see-saw!

Bull's eyes were like huge, brightly coloured pandrops and, as you sucked off one layer of colour, another appeared from underneath. This in turn gave way to a third and so on. As you had to take it from your mouth to see what the next colour was, you could hardly say it was a hygenic sweet!

We sometimes managed to have extra sweets from shops where, if you gave some custom, the shop lady handed out a few.

Ice-cream was also a prime favourite. An Italian used to push his little cart along shouting, 'Hice-cream, hice-cream'. You could get a half-penny slider or a huge penny slider (ice-cream sandwiched between two wafers), or you could have half-penny cones or a large penny cone. But we were lucky because Mother liked to make her own ice-cream. She said, 'You know what's in it'. She had a double container like a barrel with ice (from the fishmonger) and salt between two tins. The ice-cream mixture was put in the centre part and the tin whirled round and round like a butter churn. Sometimes this took quite a time, but we did not weary as we knew what a delicious treat was in store.

Another little barrow-cart which appeared from time to time causing a buzz of excitement was the jam jar man. You could see him from a distance by the multi-coloured balloons floating gently in the air. Into the houses like lightning dashed the children pleading for a jam jar or bottle or rags or even bones.

The pantomime song had it:

> Any rags? ta ra ra ra ra — rags! ta ra ra ra ra
> Any rags, any bones, any bottles today?
> It's the same old story in the same old way.

So, out dashed the children to barter for balloons.

Then there was the organ grinder with monkey dressed beautifully in velvet, a smoking cap perched jauntily on his head. The organ man knew just the jolly tunes that children liked and he encouraged them to dance, which they did with glee. At the end of the tune, the monkey, who had been sitting on top of the organ, jumped down onto a handle, took off his cap and held it out for reward. When anyone put in a half-penny or one penny he saluted smartly with the other hand.

Ocassionally there was the thrilling and exciting sight of a man with a huge dancing bear. The man had a large pole. The bear was on a strong chain and was muzzled. Although we would not admit it, we were all somewhat afraid of this monster, but there was a fascinating attraction about it as well.

Punch and Judy shows were great fun and appeared not only in the street but also at the seaside and parties.

Nearly every Sunday morning the Salvation Army had a stance near Union Grove. I am sure that many have been drawn in to hear the message of the Gospel by their stirring hymns played and sung with such fervour.

Our milk was brought in milk carts. The horses grew to know the rounds and the exact places to stop. They got many titbits from kind people. The cart had large cans with taps on each side, and the milkman stood on the lowset floor between. As he approached a stance, he blew a whistle and people all came running from the houses with jugs for him to fill. He usually had full cream milk, skimmed milk, buttermilk, cream and double cream, eggs, butter, and sometimes farm cheese.

At this time, nearly all the farms made their own butter and cheese and customers had favourite farms which they patronised. We were always on the look-out to get a ride on the milk cart and perhaps ring the bell of a house from where no one had come out.

A fish hand cart came a few times a week with line-caught fish. The man shouted out his wares; it might be 'Roastin' 'addies six a penny'. We also had a fish-wife who came once a week wrapped warmly in a shawl with her creel on her back who, in addition to fresh fish, might have smokies (smoked haddocks), kippers, crabs, buckies and dulse. The buckies were small shell fish (similar to a snail's shell) which we ate, poking out the meat with a hairpin. The dulse was first put on a red hot poker which made it very tasty.

Nearly every day a lorry came the rounds with vegetables. We could get a half-penny worth of mixed vegetables for broth! And every day or so there would be the coal cart. These great kitchen ranges swallowed up the coal!

Ash buckets and rubbish were collected by the Cleansing Department which had magnificent teams of Clydesdale horses. Every year there was a wonderful procession of the horses and carts all poshed-up and decorated — a fine spectacle!

You can imagine all these horse-drawn vehicles caused one problem which had to be well attended to. The scaffie — road sweeper — had a constant job to keep the roads clean. He had a hand-cart, brushes and shovel. Often householders would sweep up horse 'manure' for the garden.

There were many message boys to be seen. At one time our grocer sent a message boy every morning, on a bicycle, to take an order which was delivered in the afternoon.

You would frequently see a young lady coming along carrying a huge band-box. This would be a 'sight' of clothes or hats which had been selected in the shop to be sent and tried on at home. The dresses had to be carefully packed with oceans of tissue paper.

If we were going down town with Mother or visiting, we had on our Sunday clothes and kid gloves. What a nuisance these kid gloves were to me. I often lost one and I had a bad habit of chewing the ends of the fingers during the sermon on Sunday. The ends grew as hard as boards and I had great difficulty getting my fingers in again. For the cold weather we had fur muffs. I could do with a nice muff now!

Often a street singer strolled slowly along drawling out a sentimental ballad such as, 'Don't go down the mine, Daddy'. We children did not care about the song he was singing, but we loved to get a half-penny or penny to give him as he looked so poor and sad.

When the light began to fade, the lamplighter, Leerie, came smartly along, lighting the street gas lamps. He had a long pole with a contraption at the end with which he could switch the gas on, fix a match, strike it, and light the incandescent: so on to the next, till the whole street had its two rows of lovely lamps. We never tired watching leerie's magical progress.

As Robert Louis Stevenson so touchingly describes in his poem for children, 'The Lamplighter'.

My tea is nearly ready and the sun has left the sky;
It's time to take the window to see Leerie going by;
For every night at tea-time and before you take your seat,
With lantern and with ladder he comes posting up the
street.

Now Tom would be a driver and Maria go to sea,
And my papa's a banker and as rich as he can be;
But I, when I am stronger and can choose what I can do
O Leerie I'll go round at night and light the lamps with you!

For we are very lucky, with a lamp before the door,
And Leerie stops to light it as he lights so many more;
And O! before you hurry by with ladder and with light,
O Leerie, see a little child and nod to him to-night.

At Home

We had a small back garden at Ashley Road. Things I remember had to do with animals. Mother had a pet frog which used to hop up to the back door for food when she called it. Then a day or two passed when he did not come and we could find him nowhere in the garden. We thought a dog must have gobbled him up. He was a beautiful frog, glistening bright green with brown markings. When reading the fairy tale 'The Frog Prince' I always remember him. I'm sure he would have turned into a very handsome prince!

There were a few little outhouses and Mother thought it would be a good idea to get two hens who could roost in one of them and lay eggs. So, one day, two beautiful young hens arrived. However, time passed and not a single egg was laid.

A friend suggested that we should really have a cock for a time, and one day a magnificent specimen arrived. But, sad to say, there was a terrific and bloody battle — feathers flying and blood dripping all over the place. It turned out, one of the hens was a cock! That was the last of them!

Other recollections from these days are of a cat and a monkey. We were going on holiday to Newburgh-on-Ythan and our pussy could not come. Kind friends volunteered to look after him. They lived at the other end of the town in the Barracks near the Bridge of Don. We put pussy in a well-covered box which we placed on the floor of the carriage. Thus it was impossible for him to see anything of his whereabouts. He was safely delivered and we went on our way.

A few days afterwards we received a letter to say that the morning after our departure, pussy was sitting on our doorstep. We were told by our neighbours not to worry, they would be very pleased to feed him and look after him till our return.

One of our next door neighbours was a ship's engineer and

away on long voyages. From one of these he brought a sweet little monkey as a pet for his sisters. We were very excited about this wonderful pet, and I imagine our neighbours must have been a little fed up with the frequency of our visits.

When they were going out, they put the monkey in the scullery and saw that all doors and windows were shut. This worked perfectly, until the day they forgot to shut the inside doors. When they returned, the monkey had disappeared. They hunted the whole house, every little corner, but to no avail. Still, the monkey had to be in the house as the windows were all shut.

Eventually they heard a noise in the kitchen, and the monkey came rumbling down the chimney, covered all over with soot. (The fire was not on, of course). He was in a state of alarm after his adventure and did not wish to be caught. Like lightning he darted here and there, knocking down ornaments, and climbing curtains. By the time he was caught, the house was a perfect mess of soot.

One thing I couldn't forget — I'll have the mark of it for ever. Our front garden gate was metal. One day I ran out to play, clanging the gate behind me. I was walking along when something made me look down and I saw a line of red drops on the pavement which stopped at me! Then I made the horrible discovery that the top of one of my fingers was off! I ran home crying and the doctor came. Meanwhile Gladys had picked up the finger tip and gave it to Mother. But, of course, it was no use. It took a long, long time and many painful dressings till it healed. I was lucky, the nail grew on again. Though the point of the finger is a slightly different shape from the others, it is unnoticeable.

We had a maid, Jean, and, as long as we were infants, a nursemaid. I remember being taken out in a mail-cart where Gladys and I sat back to back.

When I try to recall Jean, the only definite memories I have are of her lying on the sofa-settee pretending to be asleep. We would creep up softly and, just as we were to touch her, she sat up with a jerk and opened a grinning mouth with her false-teeth sticking out. We ran away shrieking and, after a judicious pause, crept up again.

Also going with her round the corner to the Co-operative

shops on Saturday for the weekly groceries and bread. We had large, strong net bags which seemed to stretch to unlimited capacity. I usually managed to give myself a treat.

The plain loaves were steaming hot with a perfectly delicious aroma, and, on the outside were little strips which were slightly hanging off. It was a simple matter to give them encouragement to come right off — ambrosia!

It must have been hard work these days keeping families nicely dressed — starched and frilled dresses, pinafores and petticoats — cotton for summer and striped flannelette for winter. Girls were usually dressed for the winter in blue serge sailor suits and, at school, over it they wore a pinafore or pinny. We sometimes wore pinnies even over out cotton summer dresses. Stockings were black wool, tied to stays with white tape: strong, buttoned boots for winter and gymnastic shoes — gymmies — for summer.

Our hair was sometimes fixed with a semi-hoop comb, and at others with ribbon. Every six weeks we went to the hairdresser to have shampoo, pointing and singeing. Gladys had a lovely head of natural curls and it is still naturally wavy. Mine was longer and straighter. It grew so long I could sit on it. The colour was auburn; sometimes I heard it described as ripe corn.

Children can be rather unkind. One poor soul who had meagre hair, tried to make up for it with gorgeous ribbons. Behind her back they chanted, 'Penny-worth of hair, tup-pence-worth of ribbon'.

Gladys was always the leader and I was delighted to enter into any of her ploys. One never-to-be-forgotten excursion left us with trademarks for the rest of our lives. We had been about seven and six years old when a fashion started for girls to wear earrings. One after another appeared at school with little gold 'piercers' as the plain circular earrings were called, eventually to be changed to gypsy ones.

Gladys said she knew a jeweller who did it; Mother had been to his shop; we could easily have it done. So, one day, we both appeared at the shop and said we had been sent to have our ears pierced. This was done with a cork held at the back of the lobe, a sharp piercing needle stabbed right through and a 'piercer' inserted. There was bleeding, so a tuft of cotton wool was stuck on to each ear, and home we went. We were instructed to keep moving the piercer so it wouldn't stick in one position, and the hole would form.

I forget now the reception we had on returning home, but I don't forget what happened to one of my ears. It was poisoned and festered and I had to have regular and painful treatment until it healed (the hole too) so I was left with the uselessness of only one pierced ear.

Every month Mother, as also her friends, held an 'At Home Day'. It could be for example, 'the afternoon and evening of the first Monday of the month' which was printed on her visiting cards.

It was always exciting to us children as the preparations got under way and, as we grew older, we gave our assistance. Sandwiches were made, cakes made and bought, and double cream whisked for coffee and to be inserted in that delectable sweet-meat, brandy wafers. You may be sure that many titbits found their way into little mouths, and no baking bowl or spoon was difficult to wash after being scraped and licked clean. On one occasion we whisked the cream so hard it turned to butter! It was never known how many would turn up, but I can't recollect a single time that no one came.

Sometimes in the evening the party broke up into three sections. Upstairs in the drawing room were the younger musical spirits with Mother; downstairs in the Parlour were the bridge fiends with Father . . . and table tennis addicts in the dining room where the sideboard was stuffed round the foot to prevent the balls from vanishing underneath into very awkward places to retrieve.

A good few years later, we solved the problem of the vanishing balls by training a cat, Fluffy, who sat in the centre under the table.

As the balls went from side to side, so did her head. When the ball fell, Fluffy pounced like lightning and guided the ball with little paw-pats to the nearest player. So we had never to crawl under furniture to retrieve it.

For a few years Mother formed her own ragtime band, which made the welkin ring. I'm afraid neighbours sometimes did not take kindly to the sound of the band.

My Father

Edith and Gladys with their nanny

Edith (age 3) and Gladys (age 4½)

My Mother

Housework Then

These were the days when housewives who had no help, and maids, rose around 5 a.m., and often did not get to bed till late, sometimes after midnight. A maid's dress was pale blue cotton or drill with plain white cap, apron, cuffs and collar for morning, and black with fancy white cuffs, collar, cap and apron for afternoon and evening. She had one afternoon off per week and sometimes afternoon and evening off on Sunday. Often she had to be back in time to wash up the dishes of the evening meal and clean and polish the boots and shoes.

You might wonder what there was to do all that long, long day. The present younger generation would not have the slightest idea of the housework that had to be got through then. When I look back and realise how much was absolutely unnecessary, I lose patience with the slavish bonds of custom, and living one's life by what other people say.

Starting with the brass bell knobs, name plate and handle of the front door — these had to be polished every morning before breakfast. If the housewife or maid did not manage it, they had a feeling of guilt. I remember the first ones to sensibly paint them over were called 'lazy so and so's', just as the first to use long-handled mops for cleaning floors were called 'dirty so and so's'. You couldn't have a properly clean floor unless you went on your hands and knees to do it. Then you could eat off it! Who wants to? Sometimes doorsteps were scrubbed, brick red paste applied, and polished.

Tinned food also came under a barrage of criticism. You were lazy; did not feed your family properly. 'SHE can only cook with a can opener' — 'I NEVER have a tin in the house!'

The wash was huge — all those frills and starched linen. The whites were boiled in a 'copper' in the scullery or outside wash-house. It burnt sticks, coal and rubbish, and had to be lit early in the morning. At the end of wash-day you were supposed to whitewash the boiler. The tubs were deep and of wood and you had a scrubbing board and brush, wringer, and often a mangle, both hand-powered of course.

If it was a tenement, the wash-house, which the tenants got the use of in turn, was in the backyard, and the housewife had to go down and upstairs, down and up, carrying piled baskets of clothes. There were ropes in the yard, but can you imagine what it was like on a showery day? — and the soot from so many chimneys! Admittedly some tenements had a drying loft, but narrow steps had to be manipulated with these baskets. And, can you imagine if, added to all these difficulties, there was a young family?

Ironing was another mammoth and tiring task. The iron was a triangular box into which heaters which were red-hot in a specially prepared range fire, were deftly caught on a hooked, metal rod. The little door of the iron slid open and the heater inserted. The door shut with a click. While ironing was going on, other heaters were on the fire awaiting their turn. For ironing delicate things there was a smaller, solid iron which sat on the closed range.

The range, which had a boiler at the back for hot water and an oven at the side, had to be carefully managed with all the flues kept in clean condition. For this purpose there were long-handled metal rakes and various brushes. Then the dirty — and poisonous — black lead was applied and brushed and brushed till the black surfaces shone like glass.

This was not all. The range was finished off in shining steel which showed up the faintest mark. Polish, rub, polish, rub — also all the fireside implements and large fender. Last of all, the steel was burnished with a burnisher of steel rings. Alas! the more perfect the job, the more easily did you see the first tiny spot!

Some housewives voluntarily added to all this labour by having steel and brass ornaments on the fender and mantelpiece. The pots and kettles were usually iron, very heavy. Believe me, a full soup-pot required much strength to shift or lift, and you had to take great care when pouring boiling water from a large unwieldy kettle. And, of course, they got caked with black stuff from the the fire, so, at least once a week papers had to be strewn round and the pots and kettles scraped and black-leaded.

The other great polishing job sometimes twice a week was cutlery, silver and brass. Every brass stair rod had to be taken up, polished and replaced. The knives were rubbed on a board with moistened bath-brick, and spoons, forks, silver tea service, etc. cleaned with silver polish and a specially soft duster or chamois. Alas, again! When used even for one meal, stains were apparent.

Cooking also took up much more time than today. It was the fashion to boil and stew things for hours; even porridge, which we always had for breakfast, except on Sunday. It had to be boiled for ages or it might be indigestible. How horrified they would have been could they have looked into the future and seen people supping porridge after only a few minutes' cooking — worse still, as on the Continent, eating raw meal! The same went for vegetables. I had an old recipe where cabbage had to be boiled at least an hour! We would never have eaten any vegetable raw!

The chief meal was mid-day dinner, usually three courses, and nearly everyone managed home for it. This alone was a fair forenoon's work. The evening meal was 'high tea' and one course only — fish, egg or cheese, followed by home-made scones or crumpets with butter and jam; tea for grown-ups and cocoa for children. On special occasions there were cakes and fancy biscuits.

The husband had to have a larger serving than the others, and this custom carried on in many Scottish hotels and boarding houses until quite recently. I remember a few places on the West Coast where the husband had two eggs or fish for his wife's one.

The work of keeping the floors clean was as hard as any of the other chores. Linoleum which covered the bedrooms, bathroom, kitchen and living room, was washed and polished weekly, and the rugs taken outside to be beaten and brushed over a rope or wall.

Carpets had to be brushed (hand and knees, of course), the fluffs, etc. going into a broad shuffle with a cover at the back (a dust-pan). Cold, used tea-leaves were sprinkled to keep the air-floating dust to the minimum. Nevertheless, a good layer of dust usually escaped onto everything, so the next job was to tackle this — and what a tackle!

The drawing room was worst. Its walls were full of pictures, three layers all round. Statuettes and interesting souvenirs, many from abroad, sat on the mantelpiece, the piano, the cabinet and occasional tables. Here and there were racks with photographs spread out like a fan—all to be dusted carefully. I once counted the china ornaments in a friend's drawing room and there were thirty! She washed them every two weeks!

Then the plants — these wonderful, world-famous Gracie Field's aspidistras. It's quite true, we all had them — in plain green flower pots, ornate china, crowning huge chinese vases, on stands, on the floor — perhaps to hide a faded bit — on stools, in corners, on stairway bends and landings, and in front of fireplaces when the fire was not on. They were hardy and prolific with a lovely dark rich shade of green leaves, occasionally with cream streaks. Every leaf was sponged weekly with milk and gently polished till they had a satiny sheen, and they were often placed outside to have the benefit of gentle rain.

There were other plants. Mother preferred something exotic. She had a palm tree which grew to the roof and a eucalyptus tree. We pressed a leaf or two together gently and then inhaled the perfume. The snag was that though many, including me, thought it nice and refreshing, to others it was a nasty smell. A teacher had such distaste for the aroma that, if a child came into class with eucalyptus on a handkerchief, the handkerchief was immediately put in a paper bag.

It was seldom that the kitchen range fire was out. Even in hot, summer weather it was required for hot water as well as cooking and ironing. The parlour fire had also to be lit every day in cold weather, but the bedroom ones were only on when there was illness. There was no fire in the bathroom. Well do I remember shivering while dressing in cold weather and when coming out of the bath.

This was one instance when our maid had the advantage over us. She had a large, slipper bath, placed it in front of the range, and had a lovely warm time toasting herself at the fire.

The maid's bedroom was often on the top floor, but sometimes off the kitchen or even in the kitchen. Her fire was also never on unless for illness. She could not use her room for sitting in or relaxing in cold weather; the kitchen with its continual interruptions had to do. But, anyhow, she had little or any spare time and was always at beck and call.

No wonder a maid looked forward to marriage and a home of her own, though only giving herself to another slavery with no pay at all! But the house would be rented; there was no housing shortage.

This was the way of life of maids everywhere, even in manses. Parents with a family of daughters were grateful to think they could get them off their hands in service at age thirteen of fourteen. The other venue was nursing which was, I would say, an even more rigorous, strenuous and severely regulated life than a maid's, though looked upon as being slightly higher class.

The maids I have been writing of were termed 'general servants' or simply 'generals'. It was entirely different in large establishments where they had their own special functions such as parlour-maid, kitchen maid, lady's maid, etc. I know little of their doings, but would imagine they had been happier having company. A 'general' must have been very lonely.

At that time in the theatre, a 'general' was often given the low comedy part, usually appearing gawky and handless, with her hair straggly and a smudge of black-lead on her face, making stupid remarks and doing stupid things. It takes a long time to live down an image such as this. Never once did I personally know one with these characteristics.

So, the long day gradually drew near its end, and with the busy housewife getting the children to bed, tidying up their clothes and toys, ever looking for holes to mend or thin bits to darn.

Now, she could sit down — with a pile of mending, sewing and knitting. On Monday (wash-day) she strove to have the ironing done and neatly folded to air on a clothes-horse placed in front of the range. It was usually near midnight, or after, when this was accomplished.

To bed? Not always even then, for there was the row of boots and shoes to be cleaned and polished, and there was such a rush in the morning — to light the fires, get on the long boiling porridge and polish the bell knob, name plate and door handles!

Entertainments Then

I suppose, at any time in history, young children had what we call 'parties'; a time when everything that grown-ups can think of to give pleasure to the little ones is carried out. And this was the same with me.

We had many parties, some of which were birthday ones. We played games such as postman's knock, passing the parcel, musical chairs, turn the platter, blind man's bluff, hunt the thimble, tail the donkey and when a little older, consequences. There were singing games and dances such as 'The Grand Old Duke of York' and 'London Bridge is falling down'. Forfeits caused much amusement. Sometimes there was a magician, a 'Magic Lantern' — slide pictures projected on a screen — or a Punch and Judy Show.

Often there was ice cream, sweets, fancy cakes and crackers, fancy hats and balloons.

Many boys wore sailor suits and girls silk dresses, long mitts and large ribbons in their hair. Sometimes we had fans.

When quite young we were usually taken to the pantomime in the Theatre or the Tivoli. We had on our party dresses and were driven there in a horse cab. Usually it was the Dress Circle. There was always one special song the comedian sang for the audience to join in and one I clearly remember went like this:

Sister Susie's sewing shirts for soldiers
Such skill at sewing shirts our shy
Young Sister Susie shows.
Some soldiers send epistles,
Say they'd sooner sleep on thistles
Than the saucy soft short shirts for
Soldiers, Sister Susie sews.

Gladys and I always had a happy time afterwards dressing up and acting parts of the pantomime.

Travelling circuses such as Cooks gave children much anticipatory excitement. It was well billed beforehand and the great procession usually had many beautiful horses, sometimes mounted by Cowboys and Red Indians, a few elephants and their picturesque Mahouts, a band with loud drums, decorated lorries, clowns and 'tumbling' athletes. The elephants often held out their trunks for tit-bits.

We saw many wild animals when Bastock & Wombell's Menagerie paid a visit and there was always a performance, usually of lions, in a cage. This was terribly thrilling as we were so close. Attendants were ready the whole time with prongs and guns in case of attack.

I remember Humber's Waxworks in George Street and to me, it appeared a weird and out-of-this-world place. There I also saw such oddities as a bearded lady, a dwarf and a giant.

There was Hamilton's Diorama — sometimes called Panorama — which visited the Music Hall on occasions. The huge pictures were on rollers so it didn't take long to change to the next scene. They often had dramatic stories with music, sound and light effects, and occasionally singing.

The narrator, a majestic figure, was in evening tails and white gloves. He had a huge pointer. To me, the most dramatic scene was a monastery in the Alps, with monks and St. Bernard dogs with the barrels hung on their necks.

You see the mountaineers starting their climb, then there is the terrible storm with thunder, flashes of lightning and howling wind. The monks and dogs set out as the storm dies. The beautiful dawn comes up as the dogs reach the lost ones, and a soft chant is heard from the monastery.

At the Beach we had Pierrots all the summer, dressed in white with cone hats and large black pom-poms. For years, the comedian called 'Jimmy the Gum' was a prime favourite. I remember him singing 'The Saftest o' the Faimly'.

I'm the saftest o' the faimly,
I'm the simple Johnnie Raw-aw-aw
For everything ma mither blames me
An ma faither pits it on tae me an a'.

And Catherine Parr, in her glorious contralto voice, sang:

You are the honey, honeysuckle,
I am the bee. I'd like
To sip the honey sweet
From those red lips you see.
I love you dearly, dearly
And I want you to love me.
You are the honey, honeysuckle,
I am the bee.

Also at the Beach as in a few parks, there was a bandstand for Military and Brass Bands, and for many years at the Beach Pavilion, Davie Thompson's Concert Party and then Harry Gordon's, provided the finest family entertainment I have ever come across. Many first class artistes joined these shows. Greatly loved vocalist, Violet Davidson, will never be forgotten by those who heard her enchanting voice, neither will that talented pianist Cissie Stephenson. The words of many of the songs were printed on the programmes so we knew them well.

I remember the fabulous Scott Skinner playing lively Scottish dance music on his fiddle and dancing at the same time. Another famous violinist who delighted with his playing was MacKenzie Murdoch.

They had to work very hard, rehearsals and two, sometimes three, performances a day.

Many people booked seats every week for the whole season.

The River Dee was the venue for three exciting events — The Regatta of the Dee Boating Club. The Swimming Gala of the Dee Swimming Club and the Fireworks Displays with marvellous reflections on the water.

Then there were dances of course. Sometimes a dance was held at home when the carpet was either rolled up or covered with a linen cloth.

My first dance was one Mother organised for the Liberals and was almost like a family affair. The ladies wore lace mittens and gentlemen white gloves. We would be lucky if we had a violin as well as a piano. A Master of Ceremonies was in charge. Ladies had pink cards and gents blue, printed with the order of the dances. The gents had a busy time at the beginning getting their names down on the desired lady's card. The first dance to be booked was generally the last one— always a waltz — as it was the custom that this was the girl he had to see home. A popular song at that time was:

Do you remember the last waltz,
The last waltz with me.
I gazed in your eyes divine,
And felt your heart beating on mine.
Now, when the shadows are falling
I gaze through a mist of pain,
And I wonder if ever, together
We shall dance that waltz again.

The dances always started with the Grand March and Circassian Circle. This was a fine, lively dance which mixed the company well. Other dances were Valetta, Boston and Military Two-steps, Highland Scottische, Eightsome Reel, Foursome Reel, Petronella, Lancers, Quadrilles, Polka, The Grand Old Duke of York, Nuts in May, Ladies' Choice Waltz.

In the country there were many barn-type dances, where the majority of the dances were Scottish — which meant very vigorous. It was quite usual for a lad to take a few collars with him as they got such a mess of sweat!

Also in the country were Highland Games with sports, racing, jumping, tugs-of-war, Cumberland wrestling, tossing the caber, putting the iron ball and throwing the hammer. There was Highland dancing on a dancing board to pipe music, the lassies often with chests covered with jingling medals, Pipe Bands and Pipe-music competitions.

Highland Shows were always well patronised and the animals all poshed up. The horses were artistically finished with coloured raffia plaited in tails and manes. All the harness shone and glittered. You would think the horses knew they were looking their best, as the Clydesdales proudly arched their necks, and the fast stepping ponies lifted their fore-legs higher than ever! But the greatest treat was in the huge Refreshment Tent. Strawberries and cream — lashings of it!

To Greensyde

In 1904, when I was seven years old, Father was appointed headmaster of Kittybrewster School, an entirely different district, so we said 'Goodbye' to Ashley Road and arrived at Greensyde, Cornhill Road, a much larger house.

Greensyde was one of four semi-detached three-storied houses on the up-hill way out of the city. There was only one other detached town-built house a little further on, then the countryside with mansion houses in grounds, or country cottages. The brae wandered up and up till, on the crest, you could look down on a magnificent view of Aberdeen, stretching right over to the skyline of hills — the beginning of a mighty range.

It was a fascinating sight to stand there in the dusk and watch the lights twinkling out one by one, while the city's murmur hushed and almost disappeared. The light from Girdleness Lighthouse flashed on and off.

All the lights at that time were gas, mostly incandescent, which gave an excellent light if in good condition. But the mantles were so fragile, the merest puff of wind could disintegrate them. Also the bunsen burner had to be just right to get the best effect. Leerie had a tricky job to do lighting them.

One of the first things to be attended to when we came to Greensyde was street lamps; we had none! Mother went to see some councillors and exert her charm. There was an immediate result. One dark evening a few cabs appeared full of councillors. We watched fascinated from the drawing room window, as they held their meeting by the cab lights. It all looked so mysterious! One said that the only objectors would be the courting couples.

It was not long till the lamps were erected, one directly in front of our house. It became a well loved friend, the base of all our games on dark nights and a good training ground for climbing and swinging on the bars.

About 150 yards from our house, Cornhill Road was joined by Westburn Drive which ran alongside the Westburn Park, mostly used for games. Across Westburn Road from the Westburn Park was the Victoria Park, more decorative, with many flower beds and a lovely fountain with gold fish swimming in large glass bowls. All along the park side of Westburn Drive were stately old trees — to become a great attraction for climbing. I had a favourite where I could sit high up in comfort reading, and not be collared for messages or gardening. When the town was expanding, these trees were taken down and young ones planted.

There was a bandstand in the Westburn Park where Brass and Military Bands played while we could stroll around listening to the music. An enclosed bowling green was well patronised and there were many lawn tennis courts. My Mother formed her own Club and we spent many happy summer evenings there.

It would be difficult to imagine the situation of a home more favourable to a happy childhood for, going the other way up Cornhill Road were fields and woods in which we could rove, set up encampments, climb trees and play tracking games. In the winter, we could go to the top of Cornhill Road with a sledge and race down for about a mile, ending near Westburn Road.

At Kittybrewster School

Greensyde was situated practically in the country with market gardens round about. As a matter of fact, we had to go through a market garden to school at Kittybrewster. Father often used to carry our schoolbags on the way so we could have some fun.

After passing through the gardens we arrived at a narrow, winding road between two dykes — Ashgrove Road, familiarly called the 'Double Dykes'. One dyke was very high as it enclosed the asylum, and the other about six foot. We had to become expert at climbing this one quickly as, at the other end of the road, were the cattle markets. Cattle and sheep were often driven along Ashgrove Road, the cattle charging madly between the dykes. I am sure, had we not got on to the lower dyke quickly, we might have been trampled on, or even killed. If there were bulls, they were always at the back of the herd. Many times I have seen a bull turning on the drover who had a hard job getting him in order again.

We were always thankful if we passed the gates of the cattle market without a gate being flung open and cattle or a bull coming out. Sheep were no physical threat, but, oh! the mess! all over the road. It was almost impossible to get through with clean shoes.

One result of this is that, whenever I have a nightmare — which, fortunately, is very seldom — I am always being chased by wild bulls; but, so far, I have escaped by flying into the air. The frustrated expressions on the bulls' faces is really very funny. It can't be a nightmare if you are laughing, so the bad spell is broken.

Gladys and I, and eventually brother Willie, found we were very special people at Kittybrewster School — children of the headmaster. We had to try to be on our best behaviour lest we let Father down. We did not like this as we had our percentage of mischief, misbehaviour and bad marks like other children.

The teachers of the classes we were in must have given a sigh of relief when we passed on to another class.

On arriving at school, we hung our coats, in Father's room, and awaited him there for going home. There was never much time for lunch, or rather 'dinner' as it was in Scotland. Looking back, I wonder how we did not all have indigestion with the rush — no school meals these days! This is one thing which has eased the work of mothers.

But, once we were old enough for bicycles, there was a great improvement, even though they were not the lovely, streamlined, many-geared beauties of to-day. Actually my first one was secondhand for thirty shillings. At that time they did not even free wheel, and this tempted us to go whizzing down steep hills with our feet up beside the handle bars. What exhileration! But how we were not killed, I don't know.

Cycling then was much bumpier on the comparatively rough roads which made punctures fairly frequent. We usually had a puncture mending outfit in the purse at the back of the saddle, along with small instruments, an oil can and one or two little rubber valve tubes. It was quite an ordinary sight to see a cyclist 'trying' a blown-up inner tube in a basin of water borrowed from a nearby cottage.

Our school books were strapped onto a carrier at the back and we had a basket in front for additional things and messages. Lamps were lit with candles, though it was seldom we cycled in the dark.

These bikes required much cleaning to be kept in good condition as the steel quickly grew rusty and, sometimes, there was no guard over the chain. Nearly every weekend you could see bikes upside down in gardens, and industrious youngsters doing the necessary with oily dusters, brushes, oil cans and paraffin. If there was no garden, the work had to be done in the kitchen. Many's the row got up between husband and wife when a washing basin or large baking bowl was discovered under the dresser with a dirty cycle chain steeping in paraffin!

You'd never believe the thing I remember best about Kittybrewster School. It has nothing really to do with the school; it is a circus. Every year, Cook's circus erected their great tent in the Central Park, adjacent to the school, and their young daughter, Cora, became a pupil. She was in my class, and it was to me as if a real fairy had appeared, sat beside me, played with me, and learned lessons with me.

Father was always visited by the Cooks and was presented with tickets for all of us. Cora's sister, Rosa, was on the dancing pony — another fairy! All the circus people were glamorous to me and the circus the most wonderful place in the world. We often got behind the scenes to see all the unusual people busy doing all sorts of fascinating things and attending to the animals. I made up my mind I was to be in a circus when I was a little older, and Gladys thought much the same.

The result was that, for a few weeks, all our spare time we spent in doing acrobatics and imitating various turns in the circus. We slept together in a bedroom at the top of the house. The bed, in the fashion of these days, had metal ends like railings. Many's the trampoline springs, somersaults, balancing tricks, turning the cat, and tableaux did that poor bed have to put up with. We tried to be quiet, but if Father heard something and shouted up the stairs, it was the best 'turn' yet, to see us in a twinkling lying innocently asleep!

Schooling these days led to the Qualifying Class — average age eleven — and a pupil had to pass the Qualifying Exam if purposing to go on to Secondary School. All these not going forward plus any failures of the Qualifying went on another two years in the Supplementary Class where they had a very interesting curriculum including Shorthand, Business Procedure, Woodwork, Art, Singing, Dressmaking, Cooking, Domestic Science and French, as well as advancing further with the three 'Rs'.

I cannot understand the tremendous excitement and controversy these days over the Eleven Plus Exam, as it is just another name for the Qualifying Exam. Parents did not object to it: no one sought to question it. It seemed to be common-sense to find out which children could go forward one way or the other.

We had regular tests in class, all counting up to an average mark, and the final exam was the same for all schools. Any children on the borderline had an oral from H.M. Inspector, but just in class and in the nicest way. Every child of really good ability could go on to Secondary as there were exams for bursaries as well as other aids such as the Carnegie Trust.

I am sad when I think of education nowadays, the mess it is in. I was astounded hearing of the proportion of children leaving school who cannot read or write. I fail to recollect a single child of my day who could not read and understand what she was reading.

Both at Ashley Road School and Kittybrewster School there was a fine system of help for children of slow progress. In the Infant Department, the Infant Mistress took special small classes in her room thus managing to establish a fine personal relationship with the children, and get good results. And there was usually a supernumerary teacher available in the Primary Department for the same reason.

But I also knew a few teachers who were so dedicated, they often had pupils to their home. It was ample reward for them when the children surmounted their difficulties.

Edith in party dress (age 10)

Memories of Thought Reading and Mother's Spiritualism

Our life at Greensyde was livened by friends or relatives visiting or coming to stay. One welcome visitor who appeared regularly was an old school friend of Father's, James Simpson. He was an importer of pencils and called himself 'The Pencil King'. He travelled about getting orders and was very kind to us children. In addition, he always carried a few tricks. With these he would amuse customers or friends in cafes. Needless to say, we were amongst the most delighted of his audiences. But I got so clever at finding out the tricks, he always saw that I was seated at a judicious distance away before he commenced his performance.

To me, he had an even stronger attraction: his conversation with Father. As soon as I saw them intent, I sat in a corner quietly, listening with all my ears. James Simpson was a philosopher, and you never knew what marvellous thing he was going to say, what wonderful truth he was to disclose.

One time it was Christian Science and Mary Baker Eddy. I remember him holding out a hand, clenching his fist and saying ' I have closed my hand, now I can't open it'. He seemed to be struggling and struggling to get it open — in vain. Then, suddenly he beamed — 'Open', he said, and his hand sprang open.

Another time he tried to persuade Father that everything in the World was only imagination. He pointed to a chair and said there wasn't really a chair there at all; it was just imagination.

Mother sometimes got him to tell the sad story of his one true love — which didn't come to fruition. Mother seemed to get him to do anything. One time he said he was feeling unwell, in fact he had just come to Greensyde to die. Mother said, 'What rubbish', and after a course of her persuasive talk, he danced a Highland Fling!

But the piece de resistance was the time when Father planned a trick to out-trick all Mr. Simpson's. Next time he appeared, we had a few friends in the drawing room, which was on the first floor.

Mr. Simpson was very pleased to show his tricks which were really very good. Then one of us said that Father used to know a good trick. Mr. Simpson was surprised as he had never heard of it before and pleaded with Father to do it. Father said he hadn't done it for such a time he was sure he wouldn't remember it, but he could try some 'thought-reading'. Mr. Simpson said that would be better still.

Now it so happens that Father was very good at thought-reading, as I shall describe later, but this time he had to be sure — hence the trickery.

Father was put out of the room, and to prevent any chance of collusion, he also went downstairs. Then Mr. Simpson wrote a few words on a paper, showed it to us and put it in his pocket. A pad and pencil were laid on the table. Willie, my brother, went to call Father to come up and returned to the drawing room. Mr. Simpson then blindfolded Father on the landing, before bringing him into the room. Father held Mr. Simpson's right wrist with his left hand and stood silently while we all thought of the words on the paper, and Mr. Simpson watched with incredulity as Father slowly wrote the correct words. I have never seen anyone more excited than poor Mr. Simpson. He was almost incoherent with praise and asked Father to do it another time.

The whole procedure was as before with another message correctly written, and now Mr. Simpson was in a terrible state. He said he had never seen a better trick; he was sure it was a trick, and if Father would only tell him this one, he would let Father know all his own ones! Poor soul, we really felt sorry for him. The way it was done was that for some time Willie had been practising writing on a little pad in his pocket, and he threw the message down to Father when he called him.

A few years after this, Mr. Simpson stopped coming and we never found out how he died. We missed him sadly.

In the early years of this century a man called Cumberland

made a name for himself giving performances of thought-reading publicly. He was famous also on the Continent, so much so, that it was the talking point everywhere, and it became usual at gatherings and parties for people to try it for themselves.

Father introduced it to the family, and nearly every at-home day or party, we had a session.

The one doing the thought-reading was blindfolded and put outside the room. A small article such as a thimble or safety-pin was placed somewhere in the room out of sight, and the thought-reader was led in. He chose one to be his chief medium and held him by one hand on the wrist. Then in silence we all thought of where the article was. If the communication was successful, the thought-reader went right to it and picked it up, or, if it was a safety pin on a curtain or under a cushion, he loosened it and took it off. Once it was in a lady's hair.

Father became very proficient, being right nearly every time, and he could also write the number of a bank note. I, myself, could do it quite well, my best effort being when my brother Willie tried to fox me by tying the article on to the handle of the door. I was blindfolded, took his wrist, and turned right round to feel the handle!

Many of Father's friends also had sessions and the most remarkable I ever heard of took place at 9 Argyll Place, the home of William Stewart, at that time Treasurer of Aberdeen, and a fellow elder of the South U.F. Church. He arranged a test of tests to try Father's ability.

He left his house, crossed the road, went down fifty yards or so to the house of a friend who was lying in bed (with an injury I think). He went upstairs to this bedroom and fixed the safety pin in the mattress.

Father got it! I heard the story of this escapade told over and over again, and I never pass 9 Argyll Place but I think of it.

When I look back upon these days I am astonished at the absolute faith we had in what we were doing. It never occurred to us that we were acting in any extraordinary way. But, years afterwards, when telling anyone about it, I could see they found it difficult to believe me.

A long time afterwards, when on holiday at Banchory, the

company was gathered one evening in the lounge of the boarding house. We were having music and games when, to my surprise, one gentleman suggested thought-reading.

I learned he had done it long ago in much the same way as we used to. The guests were very excited and pleaded with him to go on with it. He did it twice correctly much to the surprise of the company most of whom thought there really must be a trick in it.

So they devised a plan which would be foolproof. The next time, after he left the room, a waste-paper basket at the fireside was emptied and the article placed in it. This was done in silence. Then we were told (in low whispers) if he found it we had to will him to put it on his head.

There never was a more pregnant silence than when he came in, blindfolded and took the medium's wrist. Slowly he moved towards the fireplace, slowly he bent down and picked up the article from the basket. Now the silence was terrific. We all willed, 'Pick up the basket — pick up the basket'. He took hold of the basket and slowly raised it. 'Put it on your head, put it on your head' we all willed. And he did! I think, all my life, I have never seen anything more wonderful.

This was one of a few experiences with the unseen which added to my belief in the spirit world.

My Mother was brought up in the Episcopal Church, Father in the United Free Church of Scotland. It was expected that on marriage she would join Father's church and though she did this, she never took to the plainer — and to her, a duller form of service. Eventually she was a Spiritualist. She believed in Christ and indeed said He once visited her, fondling a little lamb on His shoulder.

Many times she saw people who were departed from Earth and could describe them clearly. The most memorable of her experiences of this nature was at a seance where there was a famous medium. The Marchioness of Aberdeen and Temair was present and Lord Aberdeen, deceased a little time before, materialised and spoke to her, using a pet name and discussing very personal matters.

This occurred at the house of a sculptor, George, who kept one room specially for seances; bare except for sitters' chairs and one chair and curtain for the medium. One of the sitters was always with the medium when she dressed in a simple robe for the seance.

The 'door keeper', Albert, had the most beautiful voice Mother had ever heard. George fashioned a bust of Albert and sent it to the Physic Museum at Edinburgh. But, what was his surprise when the exhibition of the Royal Scottish Academy opened, to find it amongst sculptures there — a mistake in transit! I have always intended to go to the Museum to see Albert, but haven't managed so far.

Mother's spirit could leave her body at night and she had some marvellous experiences; one where she was in Tibet with a lama and another when an astrologer took her to see a comet.

Another extraordinary thing I remember was when Mother and I were sitting in the dining room with a young gentleman. Mother did not know him very well, but she suddenly said she saw a young chap standing beside him. She described this phenomenon fully, and our friend was terribly moved. He said, 'That's my brother, he was killed on a train journey. He fell out on the line'. None of us knew of this happening.

I have never been to a seance or meeting of Spiritualists as I consider it dangerous perhaps to open the door to evil instead of good spirits; but I have heard of so many experiences of reliable people that I am convinced the spirit world exists alongside, even through our ephemeral human life.

My Holidays at Newburgh

For nine years we went to Newburgh on the coast, twelve miles north of Aberdeen for our six weeks summer holidays. We either rented a furnished house or had digs. A few other families did likewise so we all got to know each other very well. A teacher at Robert Gordon's College, Alexander Booth, who boarded College boys, mostly from abroad, made Newburgh their holiday place. We spoke of them familiarly as 'Boothie's Boarders'. We were one huge, happy family.

Everyone in the village knew everyone, especially the shopkeepers. I remember some of them clearly to this day. McPherson the chemist, Murray the grocer, Sangster the baker, Imlah the ironmonger, and the shoemaker who held court in his back shop where he did repairs. There were usually a few worthies there having a discussion. I would have loved to 'listen in' but they were all men. The tailor had an establishment in a broad lane leading to the main bridge over the Foveran Burn. His shop was mostly plate-glass, so, as you passed you saw him, like a character from a fairy tale, seated cross-legged stitching away or 'cutting out' with huge scissors or pressing with a large steaming iron. Then there was Cruickshank's buses and Ritchie of the Hotel.

One shopkeeper, Keith, had an annual event which was well patronised. He swam the Ythan when the tide was in.

The first few years we were transported to Newburgh on a brake with two horses. The seats at each side were forms on which the whole family could be seated. Our luggage was piled on, and off we set. One joke which Father never forgot to make was that all the way he could see my freckles coming out, one by one. My freckles were to be the reason why on holidays I usually had to wear a large brimmed sun hat. Mother had not Father's enthusiasm for freckles, nor did she believe they made you any more healthy!

For ordinary schoolwear, girls had stiff straw hats with a small brim and elastic under the chin to keep them in place. Nevertheless, they were so slippery that they were more often hanging by the elastic down our backs than on the top of our heads! Boys had red caps, so if any of us were lost, Willie, my brother, was usually spotted first by his red cap!

When we had bikes, we cycled out and the others, plus luggage, could go on the bus. This enclosed bus had four horses. Mother caused quite a sensation once by driving the bus and four horses right in to Newburgh. She was on her favourite seat up beside the driver. He wanted to light his pipe but was finding difficulty in doing this and holding the reins at the same time. Mother (who had done much riding and driving in Nova Scotia) volunteered to take them, saying she was quite used to it. So he handed the reins to Mother, who got on so well he let her carry on right into the bus station. People who saw her could hardly believe their eyes.

The first thing we did on arriving at Newburgh was to kick off our gymmies and go as often as possible bare-footed. Ah, the happy sense of freedom to run without stockings held up by tapes to stays! But we had to wear our gymmies on the golf course as there were bushes of prickly gorse, and it was possible to get a sharp spike right into a foot.

Newburgh is mostly built along its main road, parallel with the Foveran burn to which back gardens run down. Eventually the Foveran circles round to join the river Ythan and the tide comes up both streams. At low tide the water is comparatively a trickle and beds of slimey mud and mussels are apparent, but high tide transforms the scene when the Ythan could be a quarter of a mile wide. A sunset then with gulls, eider-ducks, and oyster catchers in the foreground can be breathtakingly beautiful.

From the village you had to cross one of a few bridges over the Foveran burn to reach the golf course. You cross the golf course to reach sand dunes and the estuary of the Ythan. From there for miles stretches glorious, golden sand. The sands of Forvie.

All along the Foveran and Ythan, little boats were moored mostly for fishing, but at high tide ships used to sail up the Ythan to Mitchell and Rae's Quay and Store building. From there a tug took coals and fertilisers by pulling barges to Ellon. It was a special treat for us to get on the tug to Ellon and back.

The almost daily programme for most of the visitors was: forenoon, set out for our bathe, across a bridge, across the golf course, past the lifeboat houses, alongside the Ythan till we reached the sea and often a good bit further on, depending on sand bars and pools. There was nearly always a marvellous pool left when the tide was fairly well out, where we could swim and splash without fear. But, quite often, we were in the sea, usually close beside the salmon nets which gave us safety and we could climb on them and have fun.

When the tide was out, salmon fishers climbed along till they reached the trap at the end of the nets, when they used a net scoop on a long pole to extract any salmon. Often 'flukes' as we called them were caught. These could be either young plaice or soles and were despised by the fishers who just flung them down on the sand! Many fine fries did we have in this way.

Our dressing boxes were the sand dunes, and often we did not require towels as we loved to dry ourselves going up a sand hill and rolling down. Usually we had races to heat ourselves, and tracking games on the dunes and the moor behind.

Afernoon: golf, and for some, evening also, or bridge. We children went round the course with an iron and a putter. If we wished, we could go a run on our bikes, and in rainy weather there was trout fishing in the Foveran burn. We also had many exciting games of cricket.

But, oh! our wonderful picnics! Away the whole day. We crossed the golf course, rowed across the Ythan, and went over the moor by the Sands of Forvie. They are like a desert, and came into being after a terrible storm which buried a whole village. Now there is nothing but sand. At the times chosen for us to go, it was also a giant incubator. The sands were covered with thousands and thousands of gulls' nests, each just a little scooped out bowl in the sand, and in each a few eggs. On our approach the gulls wheeled wildly above, screaming out their fear. Once when there were a few fledglings, I picked up one just at my feet, to have a good look and pet it. Suddenly there was a mighty swoop and I was just in time to save my head. I never was so quick in all my life. That little bird was down and me far away!

On we went till we came to the coast of cliffs, rocks and sandy bays. One called Hackley Bay was our destination; very suitable as there was a spring of sweet, fresh water. Here, added to the usual attractions of the shore, was fine rock scrambling and interesting rock pools to investigate.

Occasionally we went there when there was a very low tide, armed with iron clicks hooked at one end (made by the blacksmith), little hammers and old gymmies on our feet. This was for crab fishing. We climbed out as far as we could, to come to the softer, old rocks where the larger crabs might be. We poked in a hole with the click and if a crab was there, he grabbed hold and would not let go. The hammers then came in handy to break down the rock so as to haul him out. You see, he might have gone in by a larger hole! The pincers were tied with twine and each crab strung on to a length of twine. Once we had seventy crabs! We carried our catch back proudly slung over our shoulders. Many wash-house boilers were cooking that evening!

Another place which meant a day's excursion was Collieston on the coast about four and a half miles north of Newburgh. This time we went by carriage, crossing the great bridge over the Ythan about one mile north of Newburgh. Collieston, a little fishing village with a tiny harbour edged with fine sand, was an ideal place for swimming and picnicking. We never departed without purchasing 'speldins', a delicacy greatly loved by all. These were line caught whitings or haddocks which were gutted, split and dried outside on racks in the salty air.

I cannot see Collieston now without thinking of the lovely little cove chosen by Lawrence of Arabia to be a refuge from publicity and stress. Here, in this small cottage near the end of the pier he stayed with his batman — at peace. Here he could swim at midnight in the harbour; here he could ride on the moors; here he could buy pies from the little shop, then stroll down the steep braes; here, for a short time, he could be himself.

Often we would cross over the large Ythan bridge and go on to the moor for a hike. It stretched for about four and a half miles right to Collieston. Originally, I expect, it had been all sand dunes and hills, but now almost all turf and heather with the one great exception, 'The Sands of Forvie'. Towards the sea there are still many sand dunes and hills. Small paths, just beaten with feet, go here and there. Sometimes a path will go right through a sand hill and you have quite a hunt to pick it up on the other side.

As you approach Collieston, it is a steep rocky shore with bays and dangerous paths where it would be easy if you slipped to topple down to the rocks. One experience I had on this moor, at a very early age (I think about four) made a great difference to my whole life.

One Saturday we had two lady friends out from Aberdeen and we went for a walk on the moor. I found so many interesting things to examine that I was always falling behind. At last, losing patience, my Mother said, 'You go in front where we can see you; no more falling behind'. So, off I set in a huff. 'I'll show them', I said to myself; 'I'll let them see I can walk', and I did not deign to look back. I kept up a good pace till I found I was near the sea. On I went till I was on one of the paths going alongside a bay. I saw many people away far down having a picnic and stopped to look at them. I also remember seeing a stone engine with a funnel chimney which I learned later was for smoking fish.

Now I had stopped, I realised I was feeling very tired. I looked back but could see no one. All at once I felt terribly, terribly tired, sorry for myself, and a little scared. So I turned and thought I'd soon come to Mum and Dad. On and on went my little feet — on and on. Eventually the path came to a great sand hill. I struggled up it and slid down the other side, but the path seemed to have vanished! I hunted in vain, I couldn't find the path. I was lost!

I sat and wondered what I would do. I felt very, very frightened. How I wished I had kept with the others. Then, suddenly, I thought of the very thing. Father had told me that if we prayed to God, He would answer. So I knelt and asked God to save me.

Well, would you believe it! I immediately heard 'Coo-ee' and there was one of our friends on the top of a hill, waving and shouting. Then I heard others from the tops of other hills.

I answered back, shouting at the top of my voice, and it was not long till they were all with me.

This happened nearly eighty years ago but it is still very clear in my memory. It made such an impression on me that, often when passing through a trying time, I remembered the simple faith I had as a child and the prayer so wonderfully answered. This gave me courage and confidence.

Had I not been found quickly, there's no doubt that one man above all others would have been notified and put in charge of operations — the policeman of Newburgh, McDonald. There was a special relationship between him and me right from the earliest times. You see, I was a wanderer, and I don't know how often he got the job of finding me. I must say, though, I was always glad to see him. He was a very nice 'bobby' and friendly with everyone.

Once he found me far up the Foveran burn fishing with a bent pin and a piece of twine; another time at the Poorshouse at the edge of the golf course, playing with the children there. But the time I really distinguished myself was when a picnic party was going to Collieston for the day in a brake. They had to set off without me, and our maid and McDonald carried on the search. Eventually I was found in the pig sty of the hotel, playing with the pigs!

One incident which shows his understanding and good humour I'll never forget. I was exploring the many little pools alongside the Foveran when I saw little fish darting about. To my delight, I found a dirty, rusty tin, and after many scoops I actually caught one!

Proudly I ran back with my trophy. I'm afraid Mother's feelings were mixed. She eyed the filthy tin with displeasure, also the queer-looking fish with spikes. She said the landlady would not allow that messy thing in her house, but that I could put the tin in one of the out-houses and see it as often as I wished. This I did.

I wakened early in the morning and remembered my fish with excitement. I quietly dressed, tip-toed downstairs and darted round to the out-house. The tin was gone! I searched every corner in vain. Someone had stolen it! Well! There was just one thing to do . . . go to the policeman, he would find the culprit and get the fish back.

It was not far to McDonald's house and I knocked on the door. A lady opened it, looking very surprised to see me standing there. I blurted out my tale of woe. She asked me in and said she would get the policeman; he would know what to do.

He probably had just risen from his bed for, as he came in, he was adjusting and fastening his belt. I started on my story and he took out his notebook. He seemed to take down all particulars and he asked me a few questions. Then he said he would do everything he could to find the thief.

The load was lifted from my shoulders — I was happy again — all was well! I skipped down the road and ate a hearty breakfast. Gradually the whole thing slipped from my mind. I did not know till years later, my Mother had flung the tin and its contents into the Foveran burn.

We made many friends at Newburgh. One, Sandy Watson, a farmer from Auchmacoy, near Ellon, always came to visit us in a beautiful, sparkling trap with a spirited, high-stepping pony. We loved to see him arriving as he often took us for a ride in the trap.

The greatest treat was if he drove us to his farm. He went by the road to the north, over the large Ythan bridge and, at a certain point, went off the road down to the edge of the river, and then actually in to the river. There, the river takes a huge bend and, at low tide, it saved a mile or two to drive through the river! What bliss, driving through a river!

At one time, when our cottage was on the road to Mitchell and Rae's Quay (called the Inches), Sandy paid a visit. There was a small garden in front with decorative railings on to which he tied the reins. I noticed that the pony had put his head over the railing and was munching some flowers. I tried to get him to stop it but he paid no attention and just went on. I thought if I got up on the trap and pulled the reins he would have to raise his head. So I loosened the reins, clambered on to the trap and pulled. That did it! He raised his head all right, but also started going down the road to the quay. He went at a gentle pace, and when we came to the square, I tugged the reins to the right and he turned round nicely. But for all my tugging and shouting 'Woah!' he wouldn't stop at the cottage and went right on to the main road. I tugged to the left so we would go in to the village and at the square I managed to turn him again. I was sure this time I would get him to stop at the cottage. But he had other thoughts. Now he knew he was on the road home, so, off he went, racing with increasing speed and there was nothing I could do but hold grimly on. As he approached the Inches road, I saw Sandy and Father rushing along to meet the trap. Sandy was just in time to catch the reins. How he managed to bring the trap to a halt I don't know. He was dragged along quite a distance, but was only slightly bruised. I had had a very narrow squeak. This finely-bred pony 'Moneyspinner' was newly broken in and was destined to go to India for Sandy's son Robert to play polo!

My only other adventure of an equestrian nature was the very antithesis of the Moneyspinner one, and happened at the Newburgh games where they had donkey rides. I suppose I had been about three years old at the time. Father wanted to give me a ride and thought it would be better if he led the donkey instead of the donkey man. I was placed nicely and we set off. Father had almost arrived at the end of the run when he heard the people all laughing. He looked back to see what it was about. No one was on the donkey, and, not far from starting point, there was I, sitting on the grass, engrossed in picking a lovely bunch of daisies. I had slid down the tail!

Another thing I shall always associate with Newburgh is kite-flying. Father developed this interest which became a joy to us all; making and flying kites. He started with ones of modest size, but his final one was huge and required two people to hold it. Each kite had a name, and this one was the 'Kathleen', the name of my second youngest sister. When flying in strong wind, the Kathleen could pull us through the water at a very good pace. There was ever a vast sky and every puff of wind got right through.

Our last Newburgh holiday was almost over when 'The Sword of Damocles' fell . . . to blot out forever these carefree, happy times. Little did I think as I strolled along to the farm for the milk what was to greet me on my return.

As I approached the village I could see the main street crowded with people all talking excitedly and rushing about . . . It was the 4th August 1914.

First Meeting — Davie

When my two younger sisters, Kathleen and Dorothy arrived, Gladys and I helped out in various ways. Gladys, being older, more so than I, she had quite a hard time as I recollect. We took turns taking them walks.

When I was about fourteen I set off with Kath one lovely Saturday. Little did I know this walk was to alter my whole life! I had on my wide brimmed sun-hat for the freckles and I was feeling so Spring-like, I gathered daisies, made a daisy chain and put it on the hat. It didn't matter if it was a little foolish as I was sure I'd meet nobody.

I was bound for 'Gordon's Woodie'. This was a lovely wood right round the estate of Cornhill House, a stately old mansion house where Mr. Gordon, The Burgh Surveyor of Aberdeen, stayed. We knew the family very well and often played with the son, Eric. The wood did not go near the house, and it was lovely to stroll along.

When I had gone about half way, I was surprised to see something white shining through the trees. As I approached, I could see it was a large bell tent erected right in the middle of the path. When I got round it, there was a young man bending over a stove contraption stirring a pan. He looked up and we both grinned. 'Hello', said I, 'What's that you're cooking?' 'I'm not cooking, I'm cleaning the pan' was the reply.

These were the first words I exchanged with the young man who was to be my husband! Coming events cast their shadows before them, for many's the pan I saw him cleaning when we were camping!

He told me he and a few friends loved the open air life so much, they camped in the outskirts of Aberdeen for a few months every summer. I went on my walk saying nothing about the tent as I didn't consider it worth mentioning!

On Monday morning, when the mad rush was on, getting ready for school, our bell rang and I heard Father speaking to somebody. Then he called me, saying there was someone to see me.

Who was it but the camping chap, smiling and shyly holding out a little packet. 'I found this glove in the wood', says he, 'and I wondered if it was yours'. And it was!

Father and I thanked him profusely and afterwards I learned that Father, being taken with the idea of the camping chaps, had invited him and a friend to come on Friday evening for a game of cards.

On Friday, Davie Bishop and his best pal, Willie Henry, came for a chat and a game of cards. Thereafter, Gladys and I both went the weekend walks with Kath and Dory up Cornhill Road. How strange that, always as we approached the wood, two chaps in straw hats and waving ties appeared like magic and escorted us for the remainder of the walk!

This pleasant companionship lasted some time till came the startling news that Willie was to emigrate to Canada. Davie wanted to go too, but his parents objected. We said 'Goodbye' to Willie a few days before his departure. There was a band in the Westburn Park and we strolled about, listening to the music before making our farewells.

It was to be many years till those two lads were to meet again and, before that time, a terrible war was to kill most of their other chums.

Now Davie visited by himself, and occasionally he and I went to the Electric Theatre Cinema in Union Street. We were also at one or two dances. Round about this time one of Mother's ploys should come into the story.

On an at-home day, when Mother knew of a good few people who were coming (including Davie), she devised an entertainment. We had a very nice, good-looking maid who entered into the game wholeheartedly. She was dressed like a gypsy and seated in the housemaid's pantry in a dim light of two night-candles, and with a few mysterious things on a table. The guests were informed that Mother had engaged a fortune teller, and they were to go one by one to have their fortunes told.

The maid was informed exactly what to say to each, and Mother made up some marvellous fortunes for everyone — always with a bit of truth in it. The whole party was delighted and said what wonderful fortunes they had been told and what a great idea it had been.

There was one glum face though — Father's; and when the last guest had departed, he broke out fiercely — 'What a mad idea — a fortune teller — where was the money to come from to pay her', etc., etc. When Mother got control of herself from laughing, she explained it was the maid. Father just didn't believe it, and Mother had to send for her to confirm. Poor Father, he was flabbergasted and had to admit it made a happy party!

What I didn't know till years after was, that Davie was told he was in love with a very musical girl with long, fair hair, and he was going to marry her! But I never found out how, after our first meeting in the wood, he had discovered who I was or to where he should return the glove!

As you can see, Mother was all out for good fun. We used to play tricks on the couples strolling along. One was to make up a parcel with a string attached, and, just when someone was to pick it up, it would be quickly pulled away. Another parcel trick was that we rolled a soft soap tin (without the lid) in filmy brown paper used for covering loaves, and when it was picked up, fingers broke through the paper into the sticky soap.

Every summer, a French onion-boy came regularly with his strings of onions. We got to know him very well and tried to practise our French on him. It was rather difficult, though, as he spoke a dialect.

One evening, as it started to grow dark, Gladys, who is a tip-top actress, dressed up as an onion-boy, even adding a little moustache. She wore a beret, thick jersey and dark trousers, and she carried a string of onions on Willie's scout pole. We watched from the drawing room window when she set out jauntily with the onions swinging on the pole. She was going to visit a neighbour and try to sell the onions to her. We waited expectantly till we saw Gladys returning without the onions. Yes, she had made it! She sold the onions and received a nice piece of bread and jam! What fun it was telling our neighbour next day!

As I said, Gladys was a fine actress, singer, and even better dancer. She attended the Dancing Academy of a famous teacher, Jeannie Henry, learning all branches of the art including ballet and Scottish Highland Step-dancing. In fact, this became the love of of her life with the constant aim of going on the stage.

Mother supported her secretly in this idea, in spite of Father's strong disapproval. At last, there came the day when the birdie flew from the nest and Gladys had gone on the Stage. I missed her terribly and it would have been even worse had I known that so many years would pass and two world-shattering wars, till we would get to know each other really well again. There was regular correspondence between her and Mother, and I was always asking if there was any more news of Gladys.

The boys at Gordon's Woodie — 1912
Willie Henry (front left) Davie Bishop (front right)

Central School hockey team — 1914
Edith (extreme right)

At the Central School

I qualified when I was ten and a half and could not go on to Secondary for another year, so I had the advantage of one year in a Supplementary Class before going to the Central School. There, at about the age of fourteen, you tried the Intermediate Exam (I suppose comparable to 'O' levels nowadays) and in another three years you sat the Higher Leavings (comparable to 'A' levels). But it was much harder these days as we had to sit the whole group of subjects at one time with certain subjects compulsory.

Another thing which added to the scope of our studies was that the Central School at that time was for those intending to enter the Teaching profession. We were called 'Junior Students', learned teaching methods, and taught in schools.

The Central School lived up to its name, being right in the centre of the city, and must have been at least one and a half miles from my home, Greensyde, Cornhill Road. All very well going there, downbrae all the way, but, oh! the stiff climb coming home! Even when I had a bicycle, it would have been a tiring rush at dinnertime, so it was arranged I would go to my grand-aunts in King Street for dinner. I am forever grateful for this obligement. I was very fond of Sadie, Betsy and Chris.

Betsy, the oldest, kept house, and Sadie and Chris were teachers. Sadie was Infant Mistress of Hanover Street School when Father was headmaster.

Sadie also helped me in another way. I was very keen on swimming and the only day I could go to the Baths, which were at the Beach, was Tuesday (Ladies' day). Until I was deemed old enough to look after myself properly, Sadie accompanied me there, where she waited patiently till I came out and dressed. What a boring, wearisome time she must have had. It was years afterwards till I realised how very kind she was.

My swimming came on very well. I joined the Thistle Ladies' Club and was Vice-Captain at the age of thirteen. I developed a good racing technique, taught by the Club's trainer, Tommy Mitchell, who became Beach Rescue. I won many prizes and a quarter mile medal — also at age thirteen. I was training with Tommy for the Scottish Mile when the 1914–18 War stopped all these activities. I had to have great determination, for the mile was fifty-eight lengths of the Baths!

Best of all I loved to swim in the sea, a little bit from shore — just myself — and the sea!

I formed a Central School Swimming Club, but it was short-lived owing to the war.

My school sport was hockey. It was with great difficulty we managed to get our team together and to practise. Of all the people, the Medical Officer of Health said it was not a game for girls, too strenuous — we would hurt ourselves, etc., etc. So, at first we located a field on the outskirts of the city and paid a rent every time we played. It was just a rough field, and though it was good pracice in some ways, it was far from satisfactory in others.

We were led and inspired by an enthusiastic girl, Silva Singer, who came from the south of Scotland. She had much experience in the game, so we owed any success we had to her.

Eventually we managed to get a pitch in the Duthie Park and we could play as a school team. But we were sternly warned not to be unladylike and go through the city in our gymnastic (knee-length) costumes unless we had long coats over them!

We turned out to be a fine team and twice won the shield from the Girls' High School — the first time they had been defeated!

Round about this time I had the strong urge to be a missionary and then a nurse. As it happens, teaching was my real vocation. One testimonial from the Master of Methods of the Central School said I was 'a born teacher', and my mark for practical teaching from the Training Centre was Excellent.

We were worked very hard at the Central School — four to five hours homework most evenings and extra essays at the weekends. The first big exam, 'The Intermediate' was held at the end of the third year, and you had to sit all the subjects at once — a terrific swot! Having got over that hurdle, we went on another three years to sit the Higher Leavings, which was the open sesame to the University, the Training Centre or Gray's School of Art.

At the Intermediate stage my best subject was Art and my worst, Latin. How I hated it! I was glad when, after the third year, I was allowed to drop it. When I was actually teaching, as a Junior Student, I felt very important and I loved the personal contact with the children. I seemed to get quite good results too.

I took teaching very much to heart and tried to carry out methods in a realistic way. We were instructed to have something tangible or a model, a picture, or a drawing for visual teaching. So, when I was given out a lesson on the 'Cat', I thought nothing could be better than a live specimen.

I carried my pussy in a small case. She was a lovely, docile cat, but, of course, must have been terribly scared when I released her in the classroom. One leap, and she was in a wall cupboard which stretched the whole length of the wall. Books and various boxes holding chalks were stacked towards the front so that there was a clear passage behind them running the whole way. When you opened one door, she ran into another portion! Books were taken out here and there before at last she was caught!

I fondled her and gave her a tit-bit. Then I placed her (with another tit-bit) under an upturned cane wastepaper basket with heavy books on top. She settled quite nicely there and behaved perfectly when I gave my lesson. I remember the fascinated gaze of the class when I held up one of her paws to show the pads and with slight pressure, like magic, out came the sharp claws!

I wrote up my method book as usual and handed it in to the Master of Methods. When it was returned, right across the page in red ink was scrawled — 'Dangerous'.

At school concerts I was often chosen to sing solos and, when I was about seventeen, the last concert of combined school choirs was held in the large Music Hall. The great organ was played by Burwood Nichols and I sang 'When the Heart is Young'. The first verse goes:

O, merry goes the time when the heart is young,
There's naught too high to climb, when the heart is young.
The golden break of day brings gladness in its ray
And every month is May, when the heart, the heart is
young.
But weary go the feet when the heart is old,
Time cometh not so sweet when the heart, the heart is old.
Life's worn and weary barque lies tossing wild and dark
And the light hath left Hope's Ark, when the heart, the
heart is old.

The second verse is similar in sentiment, but then the massed choir and full throated organ came in with a marvellous chorus-climax:

But an angel of the sphere, though the heart be old,
Whispers comfort in the ear, though the heart be old —
Saying, saying
Age from out the tomb shall immortal youth assume
And Spring eternal bloom, where no heart is old.

It was a tremendous experience for me to sing that song and hear the great chorus ending in a triumphal declaration of faith in the Heavenly Kingdom.

We were kept so busy that we had not much time to pay attention to the growlings of threatening thunder on the Continent. So, when the War broke like lightning on the 4th August 1914; when the Kaiser tore up the piece of paper — his treaty with Belgium (the country Britain was pledged to defend), and poured his hordes over the border, our whole nation rose as one to honour our word.

We were in it from the word 'go'. The poor Belgians were simply mangled and massacred. Soon, thousands of their wounded soldiers were being brought to Britain. Our hospitals were quickly filled and hectically we had to find other buildings which could be converted to hospitals. Many schools were utilised in this way, my school, the Central, being one.

But, where could we go? At first we were given lecture rooms in the Varsity, Marischal College. How would this be possible, you may ask. Where were the students? — Nearly all gone. Many were in the Territorial Army and in camp at the very outbreak of war — never to be home again. Others had volunteered. After a time, there was a more satisfactory arrangement for us to share half-days with Aberdeen Grammar School which was, according to English terms, a Public School for Boys.

Being young and full of high animal spirits we cheerfully set about helping the war effort in any way we could. Even knowing the terrible things going on in Belgium and France did not daunt us. We formed a concert party to entertain troops either in Recreation Huts or Hospitals, and to raise war funds.

Our Music Department at school also devised concerts. One was to Rosemount School for Belgian wounded. I was asked to sing a French song, which I did, 'L'anneau d'Argent' by Chauminade. We also learned the Belgian National Anthem in French. But, to our surprise, the soldiers did not join in. It turned out, they knew not one word of French — they were Flemish! Broad Scots would have been better. I heard that Doric speakers got on well with the Flemish, many words being very alike.

At some concerts we sang 'Land of Hope and Glory'. We all loved this song and sang it from our hearts, meaning every word. How sad it is that nowadays it is belittled and gibed at. To us, it epitomised all we were fighting for — all our dreams for when the War ended, to have 'a country fit for heroes'.

The upheaval of arrangements slackened discipline somewhat. I am sure it was more difficult to teach us. We sometimes had to move from room to room at Marischal College. Occasionally it was difficult to find the next room. What fun we had when we found we had actually to go 'down the drain' to the dissecting room where every experiment was well covered over!

One interval time we thought if we hurried we could go up the Mitchell Tower from where there is a magnificent view of Aberdeen. But what was our surprise to find that after a certain distance, the stairway narrowed so we could only mount one or two at a time! But having got thus far, we just had to go to the top. We managed, but at already past interval time. We looked down onto the Quad and saw great activity; teachers running here and there hunting for us. Then the

Head, Mr. Wallace (Toby to us) came into the centre of the Quad and blew and blew his whistle. We shouted and immediately started descending. But, by the time we were all on the ground floor, it was time for the next lesson!

The half-day sessions at the Grammar School gave us more time for sports; swimming in the summertime and hockey in the winter; also time to practice for concerts and to perform them. Our school work was reaching the critical stage as we neared the Higher Leaving Exam. Though the Central School was co-educational, in the first year of the War, we had only two boys left in our class — then even they were taken for the Army. One was killed, and, many years afterwards, I was shocked to find the other in a Mental Home.

Edith, in her late teens

4th Gordon Highlanders Territorial camp at Tain
Davie Bishop (extreme left)

The War Continues

A short time after the outbreak of the War I heard from Davie Bishop that he had been in the 4th Gordon Highlanders Territorial camp at Tain. He was sent to Perth for training, then to Bedford for further training before crossing to France.

From then on, the terrible casualty list dominated the thoughts of everyone, and one lived from day to day, never knowing what dreadful news we would hear. The first soldiers home on leave had shocking tales to tell of trench warfare and no man's land — but even so it was usually minimised. I was not fully aware of the great horrors until, after the War, when a few old soldiers met and exchanged experiences. But, everyone was sure we would win and everyone thought this was the War to end wars — a goal worth striving for with all our might.

We expected that Willie, who is two years younger than me, would not be on active service. He had made up his mind to be a Civil Engineer and was in the Harbour Engineer's Office. But the War lasted so long that he was flying his plane in France when he was eighteen. He was surrounded by a circus of enemy planes and shot in both legs and both arms. The last thing he remembered before losing consciousness was setting the joystick at the position for landing. Miraculously, this plane, absolutely riddled with bullets, landed safely within our lines. Willie, or rather Bill as he is called now, has still a piece of his machine in a leg. If it were to be removed, the leg might stiffen, so it is a case of, 'leave well alone'.

The War went on and on with the thousands of dead, wounded and missing. But the only overhead scare we had at home was when the Graf Zeppelin appeared. However, it just showed how terribly vulnerable a huge gas-bag could be.

All the boys I knew as a student were engaged in the services and I wrote a few of them, including Davie Bishop and Willie Henry who was in the Canadian Forces. I saw Davie the first time he was on leave in Aberdeen and I learned afterwards that the first thing he did on arriving was to visit the Turkish Baths to sweat out and scrape off as much as possible of the horrible grime of the trenches; and his uniform had to be de-loused. He used to joke about his wonderful discovery of a mercerised shirt which was so slippery that they couldn't keep their feet on it!

It was strange, though fortunate, that for all the slithering in muck and slime, for all the sleeping on muddy or frozen ground, for all the hours of shivering in soaking clothes, he never once had a cold.

It was always an unbearably sad business seeing soldiers entraining for departure. In fact, it was too much for many mothers, wives and sweethearts who made their farewells in private and did not go to the station.

Willie Henry came on leave, so there was a happy reunion but, unfortunately, it was not at the same time as Davie's. So we saw him before Davie who missed meeting him the whole time of the War. Afterwards they discovered they had often been very close to each other in France but did not know it.

Edith as Princess Crystal in the operetta 'The Sleeping Princess' at the Training Centre

At the Training Centre

In the Autumn of 1915 I commenced a three-year course at the Training Centre and Gray's School of Art which would qualify me to teach general subjects in Primary and Art in Junior Secondary Departments. This entailed day-time shared between the T.C., Gray's and teaching in schools, and in the evening, classes at Gray's: a very heavy course, but painting gave me great happiness. If I showed enough merit in my Art course, I could go on to take my Diploma of Art and teach this in Senior Secondary schools. I also went on with my voice training for singing.

But, near the end of the first year, owing to home circumstances, I had to change to the ordinary course, and decided to specialise in Infants.

I enjoyed everything about the T.C. and teaching in schools, though it was a great disappointment to have to give up Art.

As the War was on we had no dances; there would have been no partners anyhow, but we did not miss this as every spare minute was utilised in helping the war effort.

Our concert parties went on, and we had pageants in one of which I represented Canada, singing the 'Maple Leaf'. I had principal parts in two operettas, both of which we sang to the composer. Another composer, Morren, took me with him to concerts and cafe chantants to sing his lullaby 'A Hindu Cradle Song', selling the song for funds.

The Shakespeare Club, all female of course, produced 'The Tempest', in which I was Miranda, and 'As You Like It' in which I was Rosalind. Our Lady Warden, Miss Grainger Stewart, and the curator of the Art Gallery, Harry Townsend, were the producers and Mr. Hector of the Art Department helped with scenery.

Every weekend, parties went to the moors and hills to

gather sphagnum moss for wound dressings, and, of course, there was continual knitting and sewing for the Red Cross. There were also auction sales of anything and everything and on Flag Days the arty girls painted postcards to sell.

It was during my first year at the Training Centre that I joined the South Church. My first communion was a wonderful experience. I went about in a perfect glow and everything took on a different aspect. Nothing except spiritual matters seemed of much value and my thoughts were all centered on Christ and Salvation. In church I looked around on the people so quiet and decent and wondered if any of them could have had such a marvellous experience as I. An answer to this question was given in a startling way.

A large Gospel Tent was erected by Plymouth Brethern on vacant ground in Craigie Loanings, for evangelical services, and everyone was invited to come. A famous evangelist, Fred Elliot, was the preacher and I decided to go. In spite of being in good time, when I approached I was astonished to see a long queue. By the time I arrived at the door only a few seats on the platform were vacant and I was directed to one. Eventually they raised some tent flaps so that many people crowding outside could hear the service.

Here was I on the platform just about one yard from Fred Elliot, looking on the great sea of upturned faces.

The service was entirely different from all other services I had experienced. Right from the start there was an urĝency. No one could just sit and listen blandly. The prayers beseeched a living God who was there in our midst caring for us, and the evangelical hymns rose to a height of fervour. We were all transformed into extroverts, pouring out our troubles, asking for healing, and asserting our intentions to cast away any doubt and enter the new, wonderful life, cleansed from sin by the love and sacrifice of Christ.

The sermon, or rather 'message ' also had this tremendous vitality. Each face in the multitude had the same rapt expression as they listened. Even the 'staid' members of my church were touched with this magic and sang the hymns as glory glowed in their eyes.

'I am coming Lord to Thee, When His Face I see; Jesus, lover of my soul; How sweet the name of Jesus sounds; Count your blessing; Jesus, the very thought of Thee; Just as I am without one plea'.

How marvellous, I thought, if this wonder could be experienced over the whole world. Wars would cease, and love would reign. But I was brought up with a jerk when I realised that, at that very moment, millions of committed Christians were locked in deadly combat inflicting terrible wounds and killing one another — each army being blessed by their priests.

I learned with sadness and almost despair that the Plymouth Brethren would not look upon me as a Christian, although a member of the United Free Church, and I would not be allowed to partake in their Communion Service.

These happenings made me consider the Religious Instruction at the T.C. Every student was given this subject and sat exams on it. We had mostly bits from Old Testament history. I now was convinced that priority should be given to converting students to Christianity. How could teachers teach Christ and Salvation if they, themselves, were not converted? I am afraid many were very cynical, and I could not imagine them teaching it to children.

So I had an interview with the Professor who was very patient with my youthful brashness. At least, he could tell I was in earnest, but of course no change was possible.

Round about this time I had once again the strong urge to be a missionary and after much consideration and prayer, I took what I thought to be a decisive step. I called to consult my minister. He suggested that I go to evening classes which would be helpful, but I could not do so, owing to my other work. That was the beginning and end of it.

In my final year at the Training Centre we were enlivened and excited by 'The Students' Movement' which aimed at not only increasing the miserable pittance of teachers' salaries, but also raising the whole status of the Teaching Profession.

By this time, 1917, there was a great shortage of teachers, so we thought if we could get most final year students in Scotland to sign they would not accept a post with a salary under a certain amount, this would achieve our purpose. The tail would wag the dog.

Naturally, the Educational Institute of Scotland — the

E.I.S. — showed friendly interest in our proposition and we elected our President and Committee and I, full of enthusiasm was elected to be Secretary. The President was Mary Sutherland, a very fine person in every way. I heard later that she became editor of one of the Labour Party's magazines. She and I were invited to Edinburgh along with the representatives of Edinburgh, Glasgow and Dundee T.Cs. to meet members of the E.I.S. and get things going properly.

This was the first time I had been far from home in a train. What an adventure it was! I'll never forget my first sight of the Forth Bridge. And what a satisfying feeling we had that we might manage to achieve something of great importance for the Profession.

At the meeting we found ourselves in complete agreement on everything except the minimum amount we would accept. At Aberdeen the commencing salary was £45 per annum, if you were at home and £50 per annum if away from home. As during the War, prices mounted and mounted, this became more and more ridiculous.

Aberdeen recommended £80, Dundee £70, Glasgow £90 and Edinburgh £80. Eventually we struck the happy medium and £80 it was to be. The E.I.S. accepted this decision and we laid plans for getting on with the project immediately. We drafted and had printed enrolment tickets for the movement.

Back we came with enthusiasm burning at fever pitch and started a series of meetings where we hoped to arouse the others. We also gave out documents to sign, one of which was always on a table at the entrance.

The project was a complete success, over 90% signing. This was the start of improved conditions for the Teaching Profession and it is one of the things in my life that I feel really happy about. But it meant that nearly all Aberdeen students had to take jobs in England where, at many places, they already had the £80 minimum. So, for a time, I lost most of my pals. I myself, had incredible luck. Within the Training Centre was a Demonstration School where the classes were available to demonstrate teaching methods and it so happened, just at this time, a vacancy occurred in the Infants Department which was offered me — salary £80 per annum!

The Land Girls
Edith (back row extreme right)

The Land Girls

When an appeal went out for students to give service during their three months' holiday by enrolling as Land Girls, it met with a fine response. We heard that a group was required for Forestry at the Scottish Agricultural College at Craibstone and my special pals and I volunteered and were accepted. To this day one of my most treasured possessions is my Land Army Armlet with the Crown on it.

Whole forests in Scotland were being cut down to provide props for the trenches in France, so the Forestry people got busy immediately, planting young trees to take their place.

Craibstone is a few miles out of Aberdeen, and one Saturday we went to prospect. A suburban train or tram-car went as far as Bucksburn and we walked from there. Craibstone had formerly been a private estate and farm with a lovely mansion house. We strolled up the avenue and inspected the estate. We were surrounded by beauty, and thereupon made up our minds to find out if it would be possible to stay there instead of travelling out and in every day.

What was our delight to find an empty cottage of two very large rooms adjacent to that of the grieve of the farm, and we were told we could have it. The only snag was that for some time it had been used for grub-killing experiments, and a fine mess lay all over the place including test tubes with dead wire-worms in them.

Now we had to lay our plans in earnest. First thing was the big clean up; then, where would we get beds? We contacted the powers-that-be at the T.C. and were given permission to have four hostel beds as they were not required during the holidays. They were single beds, and eight of us were staying, but we were sure it would be alright if we slept head-to-tail — and it was!

There was a huge table but no chairs. We solved this problem by turning large wooden flowerpots upside down. A few more we left right side up and planted ferns in them for decoration.

We had a five-and-a-half-day week, with an hour off at lunchtime. The 'lunch' was given us by the College and prepared by the grieve's wife. All it consisted of was bread, buns, butter, jam and tea. Our other meals were our own affair and I can tell you we had many a gorgeous feast.

We were disappointed at first when told what our work would be. Of all the facets of forestry, the most lowly was weeding young trees. It did not sound romantic in the slightest. Nevertheless, it was stressed on us how important it was to have good weeders for these trees. Market-garden weeders were used to grabbing weeds by the fistful often with clumps of earth adhering, but these tiny trees required delicacy and careful treatment so as not to slacken the roots.

My first efforts showed me this was no exaggeration. It was very fine work. It took some time till I could get up any speed and know it was done thoroughly, and there was a very annoying complication.

Nature is wonderful all right, but we could do without some of its wonders. A weed growing in the plant beds looked just like the young trees. I found it very difficult to differentiate between them. This meant I had to stare so hard at the trees that for the first week or two, after-image trees appeared wherever I looked.

But to come to our settling in. We cleaned the place up one week-end and hired a lorry for the day we were to go out. Eight of us were to stay and two travel out and in.

Each of us contributed bed and table linen as well as personal belongings, and the lorry collected us and our goods. We drove out merrily, even bursting into song occasionally. What a wonderful sense of freedom we had!

Many pairs of hands soon had everything in order, then we got down to making a working schedule. We had a kitty into which we put so much weekly, I think it was five shillings, for our food and household expenses. If we went over, then we shared. One of us would be house-mother each week and would get time off to cook a really good supper for our return from the fields.

We designed and made a khaki 'uniform' for ourselves —

smock and breeches although one or two did not conform. Thus, when we went to Bucksburn for our shopping, children used to shout 'Breeks' at us. You see, it was most unusual these days for ladies to wear trousers of any kind! But it was the most sensible thing we could have done, as we had to sit or kneel for our work, on sacks placed in the alleys between the plant beds. In wet weather, skirts would become soaked and muddy.

We arranged that we could manipulate our hours of working so that, if we put in extra time for a day or two, we could all have an afternoon off when we could go picnicking to the woods or hills. Our favourite place was a beautiful hill which we christened 'The Heather Hill' as it was so prolific in heather. From this hill you had a mangificent panoramic view of the River Don, with that graceful mountain, Bennachie, in the distance. This mountain always reminds me of the Gordon Highlanders as their regimental march is:

O, gin I were where the Gadie rins,
Where the Gadie rins, where the Gadie rins,
O, gin I were where the Gadie rins
At the fit o' Bennachie.

And there's no doubt, then in 1916, every Gordon Highlander would have given a lot to be there. There's no doubt also that many a Gordon from this district, as his life blood ebbed away in the trenches or no-man's land, had a vision of his home and Bennachie.

We made friends with many who came to Craibstone on business — one in particular — the 'Bee man' who was only too pleased to let us see him doing all sorts of interesting things. We saw him transferring newly swarmed bees from a straw skep to a proper hive. He rolled up his sleeves, put his hands amongst the bees which crawled up and up his arms till they were covered. He then crossed to the new hive and shook the bees on to the running-up board. And, would you believe it! — they obediently crawled up through the hive door and got busy at once!

We also saw a new Queen Bee being inserted into a hive. She had been sent through the post from Italy in a special box which was placed in the hive. Immediately there was a furious outburst of angry buzzing. No stranger was to get into their hive and stay alive! However, the only way they could reach her was to chew through the thick wax at one end of the box. This took quite a time — so long, that all enmity was lost and she was welcomed as a Royal Queen.

We helped to paint the hives and were shown how a bee-line is absolutely straight. One hive was shifted to the side a yard or two. The homing bees flew right to the very spot where their little door should have been, then flew round in circles, eventually landing on the correct running board.

We accepted with great pleasure combs of honey which were not perfect.

Occasionally there was a meeting of farmers at the Mansion House and we were roped in to help make the tea and serve it with biscuits. These were tiny and we had many chuckles seeing the farmers not standing on ceremony and grabbing huge handfuls.

Experiments were being carried out regarding the best clover for animal feeding and there were beds of different clovers. What was our delight to find a whole bed of four-leaved clovers! Many a soldier, sailor or airman, for luck, carried in his pocket-book a Craibstone four-leaved clover.

The first week, the house-mother made scrumptious soup which we all enjoyed — then discovered she had used plaster of paris which we had used to stuff up mouse holes instead of flour to thicken it! Luckily there were no bad effects!

Some week-ends we had visits from relatives and friends and at others, we went home, arriving back on Saturday evening. We devised a special treat for ourselves on these occasions. Each of us had to bring something eatable value nine pence from town. When the full complement had arrived, we put two beds together and sat round on them in a circle. Our purchases were then dumped in the middle. We called this a 'Silly Supper', and silly it was, from crab to black-sugar strips, from mealy puddings to peas-in-the-pod! The first Sunday, we dressed in our 'decent' clothes and set off for the nearest church, Newhills, an ancient country church with some old fashioned pews like boxes. We sat in the little gallery to the left of the pulpit. There were not many at the service, so it was apparent to all, including the young preacher, that a bevy of young lassies had turned up from somewhere. If they had not noticed us before, they certainly did during the first psalm for we made a good choir!

A few days afterwards, the minister, an assistant minister as he turned out to be, paid us a visit and asked if he could bring two friends next time. This was the beginning of a very pleasant friendship. The Minister of Newhills Church was unwell and so assistant ministers were engaged. We had an arrangement on Sundays so that we would know which day of that week they would be coming. If it was Monday, the minister placed one finger thoughtfully on his cheek; if Tuesday, two fingers — and so on. One Saturday we were invited to the Manse where we had a lovely afternoon tea, and games of clock golf on the lawn.

One of the ministers showed interest in my lyrics and asked if he might preach a sermon on one, reciting it at the end. This was to be in Aberdeen's ancient Cathedral, 'St. Machar'. One of my friends who usually attended the Cathedral, came with me, but I did not tell her the real reason I was there.

We had the usual capers that young folk indulge in such as apple-pie beds. On one occasion a long, thin branch of a tree, bare except for a few rustling leaves at the tip, was concealed until 'lights out'. When all was quiet, the branch was stretched over, so the leaves tickled the girl in the nearest bed!

Another never-to-be-forgotten evening, when we were all in our nighties ready for bed, one girl, who was gazing out at the window, called on us to come and look. It was like a fairy-land. The moon was large, clear and silvery; there was not a breath of wind and the air was balmy with the scent of blossom. One girl descended to the door, then ran on to the lawn, skipping about. Soon we were all there, eight fairies dancing an eightsome reel in bare feet!

The evening before our departure we had a 'ghostie' dance through the fields, each with a sheet or tablecloth on — then up to enjoy our farewell supper.

We travelled home the same way we set out — on a lorry with our goods. Home to work, home to leave the healing powers of Nature for the depressing and tragic atmosphere of war.

Never shall I forget the sight of our beautiful trees lying

felled — even the Silver Birch — just to be used as trench props; as I try to describe in my poem 'The Silver Birks are Lying' Low'.

The silver birks are lying' low,
Their dainty leaves are witherin' slow,
Fit should be shimmerin' in the sun
Noo trailin' on the mucky gr'un'.
The Ladies o' the Forest, prood,
Wha winter's direst storms withstood
Sae mony a year; tae man's fell axe
Ha'e bent their heids. Wi' groanin' cracks
They quiver, lean, syne wrench an' rax
Till — crash! it's ower, an' a' that's left
The raw, bared stump, o' life bereft.

Nae mair wi' unsurpassin' grace
They'll don their gear o' leafy lace,
Nor ilka tender, swayin' spray
The faintest, fannin' breeze obey;
Liltin' low a woodlan' lay
While leaves on muted rustles play.
Nae mair the silvery, satin sheen
Fit jewels for a Forest Queen
Will glint a' throu' the dappled glade,
Ower which a fragrant scent is sprayed.

Wae's me! fan even they maun dee
Tae feed war's furnace. Wae's, wae's me!

The silver birks are lying' low.
Their dainty leaves are witherin' slow.

The Land Girls again

The Demonstration School

Eventually I was so delighted to have the offer of the Demonstration School post, I put behind me any thoughts of other projects. This was the cream of Infant Schools of that time. The Infant Mistress, Miss Young, was clever and progressive with an open mind for new or more attractive methods.

As a student I had taken a special interest in this department; it was so different from other schools; quite exciting. All round the rooms was blackboarding, each child having his or her own board. Some served a dual purpose as they were also doors to cupboards. A great experiment was going on in the teaching of reading by a phonic method of one symbol for each sound and no exceptions. Special reading books were printed using these symbols. All lessons were taught by play methods as far as possible. We had the gymnasium with a piano a few yards away for all sorts of activities and games. The number in a class was as near thirty as could be managed. I would have to demonstrate methods to students.

It was a one class per standard school, i.e. one class at each stage. This meant three classes in the Infant Department, starting with what was also an innovation at that time, a Montessori class for 4–5 year olds. The 'baby class' followed at 5–6 years, then the Senior Infants at 6–7 years, after which they moved on to the Primary Department.

I had the baby class. It was a pleasure to start with children who had been in the Montessori class as they were ready to settle in at once. They all loved the school. It was the happiest job I could ever have had.

I rose to the challenge of the Demonstration Lesson which I made as interesting as possible. There was no difficulty with children's nerves or showing off as they were accustomed to students in the Montessori class.

One time, when my class had made a panel of daffodils

stretching right along the back of the room, using paper-tearing for the flower heads and chalk drawing for the stalks and leaves, students said that they didn't believe the children did it themselves. They were sure I must have helped a lot. The long panel consisted of six or so short panels joined together, one panel being completed at a time.

So Miss Young arranged a demonstration when they saw for themselves that I never went near the panel. Actually it was a great compliment to my teaching. Demonstrations meant much more homework, but I loved doing it.

Teaching reading by the Phonic method was marvellous. Can you imagine no exceptions? Also it was all by sound, so any local accent or bad habits, as the glottal plosive, were evaded. By the end of the first year, average age six, every child could read anything at sight up to two syllables and most to three syllables.

But I had the best of it. Unfortunately the Phonic symbols had to be changed over to our usual letters. This had to start in the Senior Infants and be carried on in the Primary department. It was a very difficult and trying job, like teaching the children two languages. It meant that Reading, Spelling and Writing took up a disproportion of allotted time. Although the children remained fairly good readers, they were bad spellers. I myself make many spelling mistakes through having taught the Phonic method.

When a new headmaster came, Mr. Lawrence, a deputation of Primary teachers requested him to consider discontinuing this method, and he did. In all, it was taught for ten years.

So what was my surprise a few years ago to see that an almost identical method was being taught in some schools and widely advertised as a 'new' I.T.A. method!

Counting was taught by infinite variety; understanding first, and then memorising. Addition and Subtraction were taught at the same time, one number at a time. Supposing the number was four, I would have a little house and four boys would go in, one after the other, giving the concept of four in one room; or four sailing boats going into a harbour, or four boys going in a corner, or four red sweets put in a bag, or four red flowers put in a vase.

Then it would be two boys and two girls entering the house,

two rowing boats and two sailing boats in the harbour; two boys and two girls in the corner; two red and two yellow sweets into the bag; two red and two yellow flowers in the vase. Then, when the two girls came out of the house, how many people left inside? Next, the same procedures with one and three. All this would happen over and over with other things. The children also made the numbers 1, 2, 3 and 4 with chalk on boards with the number of balls or balloons opposite.

They did the same sort of thing on the wall boards, perhaps illustrating a story about four cats. Then, for the play shop, four of this or four of that would be bought, or three of one colour and one of another; or two and two — and so on. Infinite variety which is the key not only to interest but also to understanding and memorising.

I have given you a little idea of how we planned one lesson to merge in others. Drawing and clay-modelling entered into all the lessons including Nature Study, Geography, History and Bible stories. Singing and Acting little plays were enjoyed immensely. Every child liked to pretend and lost any natural shyness in playing a part.

Many people think that it is an easy job to teach infants with lovely short hours. Believe me, what actually takes place in the classroom is but the tip of an iceberg, often the result of hours and hours of planning and preparation.

Often there would be funny incidents and sayings. I wish I had taken a note of some of them. I remember two when the children were illustrating on their boards the story of 'Goldielocks and the Three Bears'. Students were watching. I heard hilarity coming from one place and went to see what it was all about. Well! there was Goldielocks in her little bed and a chamber pot underneath it!

The other was also something under a bed, something much more unexpected; a spider's web! I asked the girl why she had the spider's web there and she said, 'We always have a spider's web. Our Granny won't let anyone touch it. She says it would be unlucky'.

Davie Again

To the north of St. Cyrus are rocky headlands of bizarre and picturesque shapes. One large rock is called 'Saddle-back' or 'The Hen Rock', and it is exactly like a hen. To the south, a wide strip of green sward lies between the foot of the cliffs and glorious sand stretching right to Montrose. It was a proper seaside holiday place.

One time while there I received a letter from Davie Bishop saying he had been on leave and was passing through Montrose on his way back. He said he would like me to meet the train. This I did, and as it approached, I saw him absolutely hanging out of a window to make sure I would see him. After preliminary greetings, he took out his pocket book to give me a photograph. Then I said, 'Do you have to go in this train? Surely you could spend the afternoon here and catch a later train'. He then started to fling out all his impedimenta from the luggage rack and all round about. Finally, as the train was moving off, he took a great leap and landed on the platform in the middle of his stuff.

I had been invited to a friend at Montrose for afternoon tea, so Davie got all his kit together and came along with me. While there, he made the startling discovery he had lost his railway travelling warrant. It must have blown away when he had out his pocket book. This was a serious matter, and many ideas for solution of the problem were found to be useless. At last Davie thought he had a brain-wave.

He went to the Police Office. I waited outside anxiously and was very relieved when he appeared smiling and showed me a document. He had told the officer his story and suggested that they could give him a warrant. The reply was that they had no Military Warrants. Then Davie said they were bound to have police warrants and they could mark it 'Military'. After some demur they did this, marking it 'Military' in red ink — with other explanatory remarks. I still have this unique document.

I learned afterwards that Davie had trouble from only one ticket inspector. But this was soon settled when Davie said, 'O.K., I'll be glad to go to prison instead of France, and you can take my place there'. The inspector vanished quickly. I also learned afterwards that Davie was already late with the first train!

My correspondence with Davie stepped up after this incident and as I had commenced teaching at the Demonstration School, I had lots of interesting and amusing items to tell him.

The War, as we know, went trailing on and there were all sorts of rumours both of success and disaster. We lived from day to day never knowing when a relative or friend would be reported killed, wounded, missing, or a prisoner. By this time women were tackling all sorts of jobs which formerly they had not been permitted to do. It was quite sensational in Aberdeen when they became conductresses on tram cars!

Davie came on leave in September 1918 and luckily I was at home, so we had time to get to know each other. On the Saturday before he was due to return we planned a special excursion to my favourite spot, the Heather Hill at Craibstone. It was a glorious Autumn day and we were betrothed on the hill. We said goodbye that evening and next day he set off for France again.

Now letters came fast and furious, nearly every day, a few about twenty pages long! A short time afterwards, I received a sprig of white heather which he had found growing behind the lines. I still have it.

Davie

Edith

The War Is Over

Towards the end of October 1918 I heard that Davie was 'resting' in Rouen. He had been there a few times formerly, recovering after gruelling trench warfare. So that was where he was on the 11th November when the Armistice was declared.

At home we all went wild and I took part in a great procession. The tremendous excitement was to know when the boys would be coming home. But they learned the hard way that they could not just up tail and run home. Unfortunately, departures were not well regulated. So when some who had been a comparatively short time in France were demobilised, the poor remnants of the Old Contemptibles and other veterans of the War were wild with rebellion. They laid all sort of plans, one of which was to commandeer barges and sail home down the Seine. Thank Goodness, it did not come to that!

I remember I passed through a very anxious time, never knowing when I would hear that Davie was coming home.

One day, when I arrived home from school, I found the welcome letter saying he was on his way. He said he would meet me at a place up Cornhill Road which was a favourite spot of mine. I got a tremendous shock, though, when I saw the date. It was to be that very day, and I should have been on my way already. I dashed off in a state of turmoil and arrived just a minute or two before him.

On demobilisation each soldier was given a pamphlet which I have preserved and which I always take out and read as Armistice Day, 11th November draws near. It is not amiss to include the opening paragraphs here.

> Goodbye, and good luck, say we who remain behind for a time to you who are now crossing to the Homeland for demobilization.

> We shall not forget the times we have had together. Some merry and bright; some sad; some spent in the line, some in billet, evenings at the Recreation Huts, and talks over the Camp Fire. Standing solid in a common cause, and as good a cause as ever man fought for, we have come to know one another, live for one another, love one another.
> Neither shall we forget those who have given their lives for the cause. Within three miles of this spot there is a cemetery where lie the bodies of some 15,000 of our comrades, only one of the many cemeteries to be found all over the war area on this and other fronts. When we reach home, in every town and village we shall witness the erection of War Memorials, inscribed with the names of those whom we knew before the War as fellow-townsmen, but who, alas, will never return. No, we shall never forget. We are determined, for their sakes, for the sake of their sorrowing women that the sacrifice they made shall not have been in vain.

Yes — we believed we had won the 'War to end Wars'. This was the future we were all to strive for. Nothing less would make up for the heartbreaks, the long drawn out anxieties, the terrible sufferings. Would trees of happy life spring from the soil to take the place of endless fields of white crosses?

8th September 1920

Davie and I had many happy outings and cycle runs at the weekends. He had been very fortunate after being so long at the War, to have escaped physical injury, but his nerves had had a series of shocks from which he was never fully to recover.

Now we had to talk and talk and plan and plan. The War really was over and once again there was such a thing as the future.

Davie was a clerk in the Municipal Gas Office. It is an interesting story how he came to be so; the first rung on the ladder which he was to climb right to the top. He attended the Normal School which usually led to the teaching profession. But he was keen on engineering and for some time his father had been trying to get a place for him as an apprentice.

Sometimes Davie was not very prompt in the mornings and had been late a few times, but on this particular morning it was worse than before. A very strict master was waiting as he came in and said angrily, 'Well, boy, why are you so late?'

Davie said the first thing that came into his head. 'I was looking for a job'. 'What sort of job?' 'In an office'. 'See me at half-past four.'

At half-past four Davie was told, 'Well, boy, I've got you a job'. It was in the office of a slater near the school.

Davie was too proud to confess and had to go home to face the wrath of his parents. To add to his discomfiture, his father had just got him placed as an apprentice with a good engineering firm. Davie was sent to apologise to them personally.

While he was in this office he saw an advertisement for a clerk required in the Municipal Gas Office. He applied and was accepted. He also went on with his education at Evening Classes, one of his subjects, French, coming in very handy during the War. He was often sent to bargain for purchasing food, etc. for his unit. Heath's French Grammar was carried right through the War along with his pocket book. Also, as I discovered later, a snapshot of me in the hat I wore at our first meeting and a lock of my golden hair.

I now got to know Davie's mother, father and sisters. His father, Roderick Bishop, was a foreman boxmaker and a remarkable musician — all self taught. He could play the violin, the euphonium, the cornet and his favourite, the trombone. He was in a brass band, Grandholm, I think, and he had passed the highest exams in the Theory of Music. He also had composed many airs.

Once when the band was trying the annual competition in England, the conductor grew ill and Roderick was asked to conduct. This he did, and the band took first prize. He was presented with the ebony and silver baton which he had used on this occasion, and Davie fell heir to it.

Davie's mother was very affectionate towards me and I reciprocated. She was one of these wonderful people who was always ready to run to help anyone in trouble. She was of a very generous nature and, even if she was hard up, no one was ever turned away from her door without at least a 'piece'. Sometimes this was not appreciated and the piece would be found flung down somewhere. But when told of this she would say, 'I did my bit, that's what matters'.

She was very religious, though often her work was so hard it prevented her from going to Church and many times she asked me to play hymns on their organ and we sang them together.

The year before I was married, 1919 was a specially busy one. As I had had very little experience of cooking, I took Evening Classes. These were held under great difficulties owing to rationing and scarcities, but it was splendid training in economy. We wrote the recipes and methods in an exercise book which came in very handy as I was to go through a few years where every penny counted.

This, my last year of teaching, was also pretty hectic. I had many Demonstration lessons to prepare, and students came for observation nearly every day.

I had to give three months' notice and, during that time, Miss Young did everything in her power to dissuade me from marrying. She particularly liked my demonstrations, and I could see she really did get a shock when, just as I was au fait with some new projects, including Eurythmics, suddenly I told her I was going to be married.

A woman teaching after marriage those days was absolutely frowned upon and in nearly all other spheres where women were so helpful during the War, they had to resign when the boys came home.

With Spring time we were house-hunting most week-ends, also purchasing various items for our home — when we would get one. These we put into store, but we had to wait longer than we expected to use them.

As we could not possibly buy a house, the only other possibility was to have furnished accommodation at a price. Eventually we procured a furnished bed-sitter in a nice district, Clifton Road. We also had the use of the lounge, if we so desired.

The wedding day was fixed for the 8th September, 1920. As was customary, I left my Church, the South, to join my husband's, the East Church of St. Nicholas, a beautiful ancient church in the centre of the city. It had a lovely chapel — St. Mary's Chapel — very ancient, suitable for weddings, meetings and various Church functions.

So, at twenty three in this Chapel, hallowed by years of prayers, psalms, hymns and earnest preaching, I foreswore my maiden name, McLean, and became Mrs. David Ritchie Bishop.

The reception was held at R. K. Smith's lovely restaurant just across Union Street from the Church and was most enjoyable, but one disappointment we had was that the photographers whom we had engaged to take wedding pictures, did not turn up.

It was a Wednesday, the usual half-day of shops at that time and the photographers had suddenly gone on strike — refusing to go to any Wednesday afternoon engagements. So — NO WEDDING PHOTOGRAPHS!

Our honeymoon was at St. Cyrus. The first evening we strolled to the shore, and I'll never forget the sight that met our eyes. The water was smooth and there was a large, bright Harvest Moon on the horizon. The reflection came right across the water to where we were standing. It looked as if we could stroll right up to the moon — a proper fairyland for a honeymoon!

We returned to Clifton Road full of excitement to tackle our new life. We knew there would be hard work, but with prospect of it leading somewhere. Neither of us had the slightest inkling where the 'somewhere' would be. Perhaps that Harvest Moon had been symbolic. If so — anything could happen — and it did!

But then, that's another story to be remembered.

Book jacket designed by
Reflex Design and Print Services Ltd. Aberdeen